"*Prison Town* breaks new ground in the study of the carceral state in rural America. Fiercely analytical and with compelling personal throughlines, *Prison Town* examines Elmira as a set of relationships forged across the porous borders supposedly separating state and capital as well as institution and community. Morrell's ethnography reveals how Elmirans make sense of their changing community and analyzes the political and economic changes that contoured the town (and other places like it) to accept prisons as legitimate forms of development. In the process, *Prison Town* sheds new light on the racializing and immiserating consequences of prison building for rural communities."

—**Judah Schept**, author of *Coal, Cages, Crisis: The Rise of the Prison Economy in Central Appalachia*

"Though prisons promise economic development to deindustrialized regions, what they produce is misery. Andrea Morrell's ethnography of Elmira, New York, offers a tender portrait of a bleak place. Through the voices of local residents, prison guards, formerly incarcerated people, town boosters, prisoner advocates, and loved ones visiting prisoners from downstate, she recounts the costs borne by people in her own hometown. Painful and personal, *Prison Town* reveals how life is broken for people on both sides of the prison walls."

—**Christina Heatherton**, coeditor of *Policing the Planet: Why the Policing Crisis Led to Black Lives Matter*

"Highly readable and lucid. Andrea Morrell has produced an urgent, well-researched, empirically rich, and theoretically sophisticated book. *Prison Town* is an enormous contribution to the subfield of critical carceral studies and anthropology. There are few works of the texture and breadth of this one, which has involved more than thirteen years of research and is augmented by Morrell's deep familial and social ties to the Elmira community."

—**David P. Stein**, assistant professor of history at the University of California, Santa Barbara

"Andrea Morrell delivers a poignant plea for prison abolition. *Prison Town* resonates with her own upbringing in a prison town where her two grandfathers had been prison guards. Importantly, she demonstrates the porousness of prison walls—prison and town leak into each other, so that the prison is a constant presence throughout all life in the town. Her work lives up to the advice she was given by an activist: 'Make it clear that it's bad for people on both sides of the prison walls.' . . . Her focus on a single town allows her to make glaringly obvious the machinations of the carceral state, providing a useful tool for prison abolition activists throughout the country."

—**Pem Davidson Buck**, author of *The Punishment Monopoly: Tales of My Ancestors, Dispossession, and the Building of the United States*

"Andrea Morrell's ethnography convincingly demonstrates how 'carceral reindustrialization' (attempts to use prison construction as a means of economic development) ultimately failed to expand the local economy and increased immiseration across New York State. With a keen ethnographic eye and empathy for those 'on both sides of the prison walls,' she documents how prison work and local discourses about crime reproduced racial inequalities and ideologies of racial difference. While Black and Latine communities were subject to the devastation brought by mass incarceration, a small group of white men traded multiple forms of stigma and being trapped in brutal and boring jobs for the meager advantages of increased incomes. Ultimately, her ethnography is an urgent call to abolish carceral systems that create 'misery at all scales of human life' and build a society 'that centers the needs of all people.'"

—**Tina Lee**, author of *Catching a Case: Inequality and Fear in New York City's Child Welfare System*

Prison Town

Prison Town

Making the Carceral State in Elmira, New York

Andrea R. Morrell

University of Nebraska Press | Lincoln

Parts of this work were originally published as Andrea R. Morell, "Hometown Prison: Whiteness, Safety, and Prison Work in Upstate New York State," *American Anthropologist* 123, no. 3 (September 2021): 633–44, https://doi.org/10.1111/aman.13614. © 2021 by the American Anthropological Association.

Parts of this work were originally published as Andrea R. Morell, "Policing the Carceral State: Prisons and Panic in an Upstate New York Prison Town," *Transforming Anthropology* 26, no. 1 (April 2018): 50–62, https://doi.org/10.1111/traa.12118. © 2018 the Association of Black Anthropologists. All rights reserved.

The University of Nebraska Press is part of a land-grant institution with campuses and programs on the past, present, and future homelands of the Pawnee, Ponca, Otoe-Missouria, Omaha, Dakota, Lakota, Kaw, Cheyenne, and Arapaho Peoples, as well as those of the relocated Ho-Chunk, Sac and Fox, and Iowa Peoples.

♾

Library of Congress Control Number: 2024053463

Set in Charter ITC by A. Shahan.

To J, A, and R

Contents

Contents

Illustrations

Acknowledgments

Thank you to all the people who shared their stories and lives with me. I hope they see themselves in these pages, whether or not they agree with my analysis or my hopes for the future.

This book has been shaped by my study and work at the City University of New York, where I went to graduate school and where I have taught at Guttman Community College since 2012. In the first months of living in New York City in 2002, I overheard two men on the subway talking about their time at the Elmira Correctional Facility; as a result of this encounter, I quickly came to understand myself as a New Yorker whose New York moved across the scales and geographies of rural and urban. Now, more than twenty years later, fully steeped now in the machinations of Life in the Big City, I have tried to hold on to my life at a slower pace in a less dense place. I meditate on the words of the great singer Iris Dement, who sings, "When supper's done we'll watch some TV show of a bunch of folks who never heard of Idaho, where easy's gettin' harder every day." Iris's ode to rural working-class life reminds me to center people, Upstate and here in Brooklyn, whose lives are judged by the powerful to be irrelevant and unimportant. I extend my gratitude to the many young people from across New York State who wrote to me and chatted me up about my research and hopes for a better future. I am grateful for Professor Leith Mullings, who in her steadiness and clear moral courage pushed me to keep going in those awkward moments where I was ready to give up on graduate school. May her memory be a blessing. Two pieces of writing by Ruth Wilson Gilmore and Craig Gilmore were my North Stars when I first started this project. Ruth Wilson Gilmore's 1999 article, "Globalization and US Prison Growth: From Military Keynesianism to Post-Keynesian Militarism" pushed my historical and theoretical understanding of New York State in crucial directions—it gave me a way forward. A comic written and illustrated by Craig Gilmore and Kyle Pyle in 2005, *Prison Town: The Real Cost of Prisons*, quite literally taught me what I was looking at when I began my fieldwork in Elmira. I am grateful for their lifetimes of work in social movements against prisons and their clear guiding analysis.

Thank you to Erin Martineau for her editing and convincing me there was indeed a book here. Special thanks to Carolina Bank Muñoz for teaching me how to be a CUNY professor and to Karen Miller whose boundless positivity got me through some tough writing moments. A million thank yous to Karen G. Williams for organizing and maintaining our writing group and helping me work through all the brain chatter to reach the other side, and to Maggie Dickinson, Akissi Britton, and Javiela Evangelista for being three more reasons I kept going. Thank you to Aisha Khan, who quickly read the manuscript of my book and became a friend. Thank you to Carrie Lane for welcoming the book into the Anthropology of Contemporary North America series and her always kind guidance. Thank you to Rachel Dworkin, archivist at the Chemung County Historical Society, who assisted me with photographs and historical documents. Thank you to all the kind and competent editors and staff at the University of Nebraska Press, including Bridget Barry, Emily Casillas, Kayla Moslander, and terrific copyeditor Irina du Quenoy.

Thank you to the many communities that have nourished my writing and thinking, including: Guttman Community College writing groups, the Faculty Fellowship for Publication at CUNY, the Center for Place, Culture, and Politics Faculty Fellowship, an NEH Borderlands Seminar at LaGuardia Community College, and, in the book's early formation, endless semesters of writing groups in the CUNY Graduate Center's Department of Anthropology. Sessions with anthropologists Pem Buck, Melissa Burch, Orisanmi Burton, Damien Sojoyner, Ruth Gomberg, Emily Steinmetz, Joshua Dubler, and Kristin Doughty nourished my writing and my ideas. In 2016 Jack Norton asked me to be a part of a panel on rural prison expansion at the American Studies Association conference and introduced me to the Critical Prison Studies Caucus. CPSC members have been crucial for my understanding of the carceral state, including Anne Bonds, Jordan Camp, Christina Heatherton, Rebecca Hill, Jack

Norton, Lydia Pelot-Hobbes, Sylvia Ryerson, Yalile Suriel, Grace Watkins, Judah Schept, David Stein, and many more whose work I have read but have never had the opportunity to meet in person. Thank you to the abolitionist reading group, particularly Lucien Baskin and Bryan Welton, for creating space to think and read together. Thank you to my students and colleagues at Guttman Community College, including, Claire King, Vivian Lim, Karla Fuller, Naveen Seth, Kristina Baines, Lori Ungemah, Alia Tyner-Mullings, and April Burns. Thank you to my friends, family, colleagues, and comrades who make my life full: Alexis Dorval, Amy Miller, Andy Newman, Beth Green Larin, Betsy Esch, Carrie Eagles, Chris Caruso, David Roediger, Dawn Plummer, Debrah Kaiser, Diana Polson, Eileen Findlay, Emily Drabinski, Kate Lehman Moon, Laura Liu, Liz Theoharis, Lynn Horridge, Mariam Habib, Meredith Kolodner, Michael Polson, Mick Rice, Mike McNamara, Sara Forgione, Suzanne Durocher Sawyer, Theresa Parrino, Tina Habib, Tina Lee, and Willie Baptist.

I am grateful to my parents, Carole and Mike Morrell, for teaching me discipline, focus, and balance; thank for your curiosity, generosity, enduring commitment to our family, and literally everything I hold dear. Thank you to my sisters and brother, Amy Slaughter, Kathleen Morrell, and Dan Morrell, for being great friends and sharing life's ups and downs. Now that I am done with the book, I hope my wordle and crossword streaks improve. Thank you to my mother- and father-in-law, Janet and Leslie Fraidstern, who provided innumerable hours of care for my kids, which brings a lifetime of gifts. Thank you to all the incredible childcare providers and teachers at the Brooklyn New School for their care of my children so that I had time to write and think and so did they.

I have received grants from the American Council for Learned Societies, the Wenner-Gren Foundation, the Irving Horowitz Foundation for Social Policy, and PSC-CUNY to complete this work.

To the love of my life, Josh Fraidstern, and our kids Aspen and Rosaleen—you are more than I could have ever hoped for.

Prison Town

Introduction

Atop a large hill in the center of the East Side of Elmira, a small, multi-racial city of just under twenty-six thousand people located in central New York, sits the Elmira Correctional Facility (ECF). The prison is a stately, red brick building, surrounded by a twelve-foot, razor-wire fence. In front of it is a two-tiered parking lot full of pickup trucks and SUVs, used both by staff and by families coming to visit their loved ones. Just west of the building, still enclosed behind the prison wall but away from the main street, are vast acres of land used by the prison for farming and recreation. To the east, just at the edge of the prison parking lot, sits a yellow prefabricated double-wide trailer, serving as a small "hospitality center" where weekend visitors first enter the prison bureaucracy as they wait for their visit. On Saturday afternoons, men, women, and children (but mostly women) arrive from around the state, by bus and by car, and fill the trailer. Women fix their hair and makeup, adjust their clothing, and, in accordance with prison regulations, remove their underwire bras. Some have a cup of coffee and a cigarette after a long ride on the bus. In the winter, the lawn leading up to the prison from the trailer is decorated with large wooden letters spelling out "We Wish You a Merry Christmas." On weekends, Melissa drives elderly and disabled visitors to the top of the steps.[1] But most of the time, when visitors are called from the little yellow trailer, they walk up the hundreds of stairs to the front door of the prison. At the end of visiting hours, or a day's shift, vehicles descend the hill, turning onto a quiet, tree-lined street running through a residential neighborhood of single-family homes, driveways, and lawns.

The function of the prison is to lock people "away," but away is, of course, also a place. This book is about Elmira, New York, one such "away" place, a place of confinement—both in the steel walls and barred cages of the ECF and, until its closure in March 2022, the Southport Correctional Facility—and a place with green, leafy streets and the daily routines of small-city life. I argue that despite the barriers aimed at separating incarcerated men from free Elmira, the prison extends far beyond its walls, with the flow of ideas and money and a gamut of relationships intricately connecting the two. This is the primary argument of my book: the prison, as an arbiter of human relationships, seeps into our lives in mundane moments and practices. In the homemade foods brought into prison waiting rooms, the care given by doctors at private hospitals for state prisoners, and the stench of prison brutality brought home to children and sweethearts, the prison becomes a part of how we live.[2] Looking at the daily lives of prison guards, incarcerated men, and their families in the context of the political economy of New York State, we see that the prison is porous, with portals and spaces for circulation and exchange. I show how the expansion of the prison as a site of racialized, gendered, and classed exclusion and dispossession has leaked and continues to leak into the city of Elmira and the wider region of New York State.

Thirty-nine new prisons were built in Upstate New York between 1971 and 2000, one of them in Chemung County, where Elmira is the county seat. In the thirty years following the Attica Rebellion, the number of people incarcerated in New York State prisons jumped from 11,900 in 1971 to its height of nearly 70,000 men and women in 1999. Since then, this number has dropped precipitously to 32,750 people incarcerated in NYS prisons in 2024.[3] The numbers of people in prison on a national scale is also dropping, albeit at a much slower rate, though the count remains nearly five times higher than it was in 1980.[4] Taken together, despite recent reductions, these numbers represent a staggering growth in the punitive functions of the state government. As a work of ethnography, my book in part argues that to understand how expansion took root, how it was organized, and how it maintains itself, one must understand the tasks people took up in their everyday lives as workers, partners, citizens, and neighbors in order to survive in, build, and maintain particular prisons in particular places.

TABLE I. Population of New York state prisons, 1971–2021

YEAR	POPULATION
1971	11,928
1976	17,705
1981	25,494
1986	38,641
1991	57,862
1996	69,709
2001	67,534
2006	63,315
2011	55,436
2016	50,716
2021	31,412

Source: Created by the author. Compiled from U.S. Bureau of Justice Statistics.

The second, inextricable argument that forms the foundation of this book is that the state's economic development agencies proposed, advertised, and supervised the construction of a new state prison in Elmira as a job creation program, or what I call *carceral reindustrialization,* as way to move public capital into impoverished rural areas and small towns of New York. I root this argument in the Marxist tradition of political economy in anthropology: that is, to understand the crisis of deindustrialization, you must examine the relationships between the wealthy governors and the working classes at the dawn of neoliberalism. The Department of Corrections in New York State—or more abstractly, just the "state"—was connected in 1985 (as it is now) to the interests of real estate and business elites to create projects that uphold the status quo of NYS as a place of investment, namely of state construction grants underwritten by JP Morgan Chase and other large private banks through which public capital circulates. Prisons exist not as places of rehabilitation and positive social pressure but as outposts of state control that also govern family relationships and labor markets in rural and urban places across the state, and sometimes, across national borders. In *Prison Town,*

I extend this analysis ethnographically. Building on my first theme of the porousness of the prison's brutality, I argue that recent analyses of prison expansion as successful sources of development for poor places fail to address the prison as a *source* of immiseration for all New Yorkers who are incarcerated and/or work in them.[5]

This brings me to my third theme: the expansion of the carceral state in New York State and in Elmira in particular has cultivated racial differences through the expansion, contraction, and differentiation of access to work, freedom, and life that are part of the necessarily unequal nature of capitalism. Centering the production of racial differences through labor *and* alienation from the ability to labor, I analyze prisons as a force in the production of whiteness in the labor market. In the case of Elmira, these institutions immobilize one group—mostly Black and Latino/a/x men and poor whites from cities throughout New York State—while simultaneously increasing the political-economic power of the state and a small group of mostly white men who work as correction officers (or "prison guards," in the more colloquial term). These workers gain a racial attachment to the state in their role as "the good guys"—the guys on the right side of the bars and on good terms with the state, the guys who are not criminals. Based on this case, I argue that whiteness is a shifting and contingent project that grows through the expansion of prisons.

Who Benefits from Prison Expansion?

In 1980, before the worst job losses of the decade, 17.5 percent of Elmirans lived in poverty. More than forty years later, this is true of 32 percent of Elmirans—twice the rate of the surrounding county and twice the national average. Elmira is not, and never has been, the all-white small town of American fantasy: at the time of writing, the population is 75 percent white, 10 percent Black, 6 percent Latino/a/x, and 9 percent mixed race.[6] Elmirans, too, have been swept up as refuse of the carceral state. Since 1982, Chemung County has nearly doubled its rate of admissions to state prisons, sending people to prison at a rate of 160 percent of the state median.[7] Overall, Elmira fits the pattern described by Gregory Hooks wherein prisons have not expanded local economies and may even be a source of economic loss.[8]

This may seem counterintuitive. Indeed, in recent years, some scholars have argued that prison towns have *benefited* from prisons being sited in their towns. In his analysis of a prison town in the rural South, sociologist John Eason argues that an Arkansas town on the Mississippi River Delta engaged in prison construction as "stigma management," assigning a "good" to prison expansion that he argues is absent from the dominant literature on this phenomenon. "Prison proliferation moreover benefits blacks and Latinos by providing employment as corrections officers," writes Eason, noting that Black city council members benefited most significantly from the new prison in the town he studied.[9] The crux of Eason's cynical argument is that the growth of the middle class through prison expansion—which he measures as a few dozen salaried jobs and a mayorship for a Black resident of Forrest City, Arkansas—is a reasonable social good; he comes to this conclusion without ever considering the truncated lives of thousands of Arkansans incarcerated in the shiny new prisons. Is what's good for the town elites good for all the people of Arkansas? Eason's ethnography falls squarely in the realm of community studies, once considered the hallmark of anthropology, which concentrates on the processes of creating and maintaining social cohesion. His fieldwork, which focused on municipal workers and "well-respected" members of the Forrest City community, reflects this analytic choice. However, since the 1960s, anthropologists have contributed to a more complex notion of "community," toward an understanding of community as a locus of political struggle and global interconnection through the study of community politics. *Prison Town* builds on this more recent body of anthropological literature, which has examined how communities oppose and accommodate changes to political economic landscapes, demonstrating how relationships of power, dominance, and resistance are produced and reproduced in everyday life.

Rather than looking for "good" in prison expansion solely at the scale of municipal life, this book asks: What do prisons *do*? Thinking of all places as unequal, it asks: Which groups does prison expansion benefit, and how is this benefit measured? As I seek to answer these questions, my study is guided by the anthropological tradition of political economy which understands individual actors in the context of the classes, racialized groups, geographies, genders, and political regimes to which they belong, making decisions in a global economy that never stops moving.

Anthropology and Political Economy

In the tradition of political economy in anthropology, scholars have sought to show how people take up everyday tasks in making their worlds and do so in complex structures of class and power. Anthropologist Leith Mullings summarizes the study of political economy in anthropology using a passage from Marx's *Eighteenth Brumaire*: "We make our own histories, but not in the conditions of our own choosing."[10] This phrase encapsulates the tensions of anthropologies steeped in the Marxist tradition: How much do the powerful make our world for us, and how do we make it for ourselves? To study the prison is to study the state: its breadth and power, its structure and its bureaucracies, its arsenal, its methods of punishment and coercion.[11] Ethnographic work in the tradition of political economy requires that we hold both of these scales of analysis together, at the same time, in the same view. In *Prison Town*, I focus on how the prison is made and remade every day through the actions people take up as workers and citizens, without losing sight of the behemoth of power held by the state. Doing so allows us to see the prison town as a place where people may be controlled by the carceral state—or may be the human mechanisms through which the state is enacted, club in hand. Ethnography must, wrote anthropologist Roseberry, look at the larger "landscape of hegemony," as these reveal "a process of domination that shapes both 'the state' and 'popular culture.'"[12] We see this, for example, in the association of Blackness with criminality and in the popular uprisings of Black Lives Matter, which constitute a significant rupture with the popular ideologies of American liberal democracy: innocent until proven guilty, equal protection under the law, and the right to freedom of movement. My ethnography focuses on this and other such moments of rupture, encompassing popular ideas about dangerous others, a powerful centralized apparatus of guns and cages, and the daily efforts of prison staff, parole officers, police, and prosecutors who take up the work of carceral state-making, both inside and outside the prison walls.

The carceral state is the state at its most coercive, characterized by cement and steel bars, cuffs, batons, and an arsenal of weapons held by police, parole officers, and prison wardens to maintain control over those members of society deemed in need of containment. And while there are infrastructures to professionalize guards and protocols for caging and dominating incarcerated people, prisoners and prison guards are sentient beings who carry on social lives and maintain political entanglements that "leak" outside the physical boundaries of the prison. Studying the prison town reveals that—unlike Loic Wacquant's enmeshed ghetto or Erving Goffman's total institution—the carceral state both is spatially grounded and has porous social borders. It is a process of state-making, rather than a static fact.[13] The barrel of a gun and the steel bars, the correction officers and their access to the state's arsenal of weapons: all these are part of the massive infrastructure and concerted activity required in order to maintain the prison. The carceral state is and must be constructed and reconstructed, brick by brick, cage by cage, count by count.

Elmira and the "Business of Captivity"

In 1876, following its use as a brutal Civil War prison camp, Elmira's first prison became the nation's first reformatory. The fabled warden of the Elmira Reformatory Zebulon Brockway emphasized a strict regimen of manual labor and "moral" training, a regimen maintained by brutal beatings and solitary confinement.[14] According to one text used in criminology courses, "Elmira's premises—individual treatment, the indeterminate sentence, and parole—were universally embraced and would not be seriously questioned until the 1970s, when a new concern for individual liberties and due process would begin to chisel away at the rehabilitative ideal."[15] Warden Brockway embodied the connection between the prison and the town, as he simultaneously served as the mayor of Elmira. Over the following century, correction came to outweigh reform, and in 1970 the prison was unceremoniously renamed the Elmira Correctional Facility.

Like so many other poor, rural, and small-town places, Elmira has always played the geographical and social role of the necessary and unwanted place in the uneven development of capitalism. This community has been a prison town for nearly as long as it has been a town, its existence fueled by what one local historian has called "the business of captivity," a place useful for both its proximity and distance from places of greater prestige or economic importance. In 1861, Elmira was first named a Union Army military depot; the barracks built to accommodate this designation were abandoned a few years later and in 1864 the depot was transformed into a prison camp where eight thousand to ten thousand Confederate soldiers were held on the banks of the Chemung River. As already indicated, in 1876, a decade after the end of the war and the closure of the camp, Elmira became the home of the country's first reformatory, heralding a new era in the nation's purpose and methods of incarceration.[16] For the next one hundred years, with the city growing rapidly in and through its bustling industrial economy, the prison remained a stable part of the city. A second prison, the Southport Correctional Facility, was completed in 1988. In 1991, three years after Southport Correctional Facility was built, it was converted to one of the state's two "Supermax" facilities—where all prisoners were held in solitary confinement. Three decades later, there are 1,222 incarcerated men living within the city limits of Elmira at the ECF; prior to March 2022 when the second prison closed, 800 more lived at the Southport facility.[17] Prior to the closure, 38 percent of the Black adult male population of Chemung County was incarcerated. Elmira thus serves as an appropriate site through which to understand the political, social, and economic processes through which the carceral state is expanded into a specific place.

Crucially for my argument in this book, from the turn of the twentieth century through the postwar period Elmira had a burgeoning industrial economy parallel to its role as an outpost of social control. But beginning in the 1970s, many of the employers who had been the anchor of working-class life in Elmira had moved abroad or to the U.S. South. By the fall of 1985, the cover of the *New York Times* asserted that "perhaps no other small city in the Northeast provides a more vivid example of how American manufacturing has declined" than Elmira.[18] The Southside of Elmira, once the more comfortable home of many working-class Elmirans, came to be marked by empty storefronts and sagging porches.

Across New York State, places that requested state monies for economic development in the face of deindustrialization were "awarded" prisons, a pattern that was repeated across the Upstate region in Ogdensburg,

Malone, and Auburn.[19] Cities that had been founded and had grown on manufacturing, mining, or farming work struggled to reorganize in the wake of a shifting economy, and Elmira was no exception. For cities and their residents to continue to be of use in a capitalist society, many places have had to become, or at least market themselves as, different kinds of places. In this increasingly competitive, globalized world, writes geographer David Harvey, "urban governments had to be much more innovative and entrepreneurial, willing to explore all kinds of avenues through which to alleviate their distressed condition and thereby secure a better future for their populations."[20] While such entrepreneurial efforts were by no means totally successful, after the decrease of federal funds to cities in 1972 there were very few options. Cities could specialize in tourism, media, or technology, with local governments providing support for businesses, but there remained a high level of competition among places to attract capital.[21]

In general terms, cities across the United States that had organized around Fordist industrialization were left bankrupt and desperate in its wake. A pattern of prison expansion as a solution to the crises of the era took root at the federal level. In New York State, the prison population grew by 400 percent over a period of twenty years. At the same time, the state's manufacturing sector restructured and the local elite of many small Upstate cities and towns sought out one of then-Governor Mario Cuomo's new prisons as a solution to their problems. Cuomo, a Democrat, had outlined his vision for America as the keynote speaker at the Democratic National Convention in 1984. Under his direction, the New York State Urban Development Corporation (UDC), launched a project to use prison expansion as an engine for economic development in the state's deindustrializing urban regions.[22] Seeing the statewide plan to build prisons, the local elite of many cities and towns across New York State begged for a new prison to "help" their economy. By bringing public monies to municipalities in distress, the construction of prisons emerged as a "solution" to the problems of deindustrialization and political economic crisis.

But prison towns should not be considered winners of a prized form of economic development; prisons cannot and have not "saved" Elmira and returned it to the supposed glory days of full employment in the factories. Elmira as a municipality remains poor. A full quarter of the city's 2022 budget came from the federal monies aimed at pandemic relief, monies that were slated to dry up as quickly as they appeared.[23] True, I found prison workers and local politicians somewhat defensive about the prisons' value to Elmira. "Without the prisons," the local refrain goes, "there would be no jobs at all." And yet, the jobs provided by the two prisons have not created a stable economy with good wages for all. Moody's, the company that measures municipal financial viability for securing loans, noted in 2019 that Elmira, along with only one other municipality in the country (Danville, Illinois), had never recovered from the 2008 recession. While the rest of the country had a net increase in the number of jobs since 2010, Elmira had lost three thousand paid positions.[24]

In brief, neither Elmira as a place nor Elmirans as a group have gained much materially from the city's status as a prison town. First, at an earlier time of job loss and economic crisis—roughly 1980 to 1990—the construction of prisons relied on small influxes of capital, which created a veneer of growth and abundance that strengthened the hegemony of local elites. Second, 96 percent of the custodial staff at the ECF and the Southport Correctional Facility are white men. While this group is small in absolute numbers, the growth in Elmira's corrections industry expanded the group of well-paid white workers in law enforcement who tend to support conservative political machines and align with pro-business development, with little or no benefit extended to other groups in the municipality. As this book will show, this development resonates with Gilmore's argument that the primary work of the prison is extractive: what a prison *does* in society—rather than punish or rehabilitate or sequester—is continue to racialize people, to obstruct their ability to work and live and thrive, while creating the conditions in which large amounts of capital can circulate with greater ease.[25]

What Was Fordism and What Came Next?

Fordism was a style of organization of the workplace that created the condition for mass production of cars through specialization on an assembly line, expanded managerial control, and made possible higher than average wages. It came with the clear understanding that this shift in the organization required parallel shifts in social organization.[26] In his analysis of Fordism, Harvey quotes Italian theorist Antonio Gramsci's notion that the Fordist organization of work was a new form of "living and of thinking and feeling life."[27] Now, in the aftermath of Fordism, we see the deep legacy of this specific organization of work and life, which came to its fullest fruition in the postwar period. Despite its breakdown, the Fordist past remained critical in shaping the expectations of what should replace it. For example, in their work on post-Fordism in Italy, Andrea Muehlebach and Nitzan Shoshan argue that memories of Fordism "continue to bring forth powerful affective attachments," particularly "the promise of relative economic security and well-being, plausible middle-class aspirations" that existed for some workers.[28] For an unevenly advantaged group of workers, Fordism meant access to relative stability; thus, the endurance of such affections is not entirely surprising. In the case of Elmira, the ghosts of Fordism continue to give an (albeit unstable) architecture to the hopes, dreams, and expectations of many working-class New Yorkers, as well as those of the governments that structure their futures.

The expansion of prisons was, for the boosters of prison expansion, a mechanism to try and capture a period of expanded wealth—if not also expanded exploitation—for working people. Constructing prisons was imagined to be a way to replicate what Pappas has called a "fragile affluence."[29] The expansion of the carceral state in New York was a process equally political and economic, involving building infrastructures, hiring upstate labor, disempowering downstate labor, and transferring funds from state coffers to institutions of punishment. This process occurred parallel to and dialectically with the loss of wages experienced by most of the working class as the economy shifted to post-Fordism, a period where Fordist-style jobs were either sent to other countries or automated while service industries grew. The crises of post-Fordism—of revenue, redistribution, and working-class loss—emerged through the same racialized mechanisms that supported its development.[30] A key characteristic of Fordism was the division, often along racial lines, of the working class into a protected class of "skilled workers" who could count on stable labor contracts and a more precarious group of people left outside of this deal.[31] As historian Laura Renata Martin writes,

"Fordism was not just about a particular relationship between labor and capital, but about the relationships and divisions between working-class people themselves."[32] And those divisions persisted after Fordism. In Elmira, the white men who had made up the bulk of the well-paid Fordist working class were recruited into prison work; they were construed as the men who didn't want to receive "municipal welfare" but were in search of "good" work.[33]

The post-Fordist period has been marked by the flexibility of processes of accumulation and the shift of economic and social risk onto the working classes; we are less likely to make decent wages, to be protected by unions, and to be able to own a home.[34] These new patterns of production and new forms of dispossession are coupled with a reordering of racial inequalities, of which the expansion of the carceral state forms an essential component.

The Wages of Whiteness?

In 2008, 97 percent of the corrections officers at Elmira and Southport Correctional Facilities were white men.[35] In 2016, the New York State prison population was 75 percent Black and Latino/a/x, hailing from all over the state, but particularly from New York City, Rochester, and Syracuse.[36] Across the United States, Black people are overrepresented not only as prisoners but also as prison workers: in 2015, they comprised roughly 13 percent of the U.S. population but made up 25.5 percent of security personnel in prisons and jails.[37] The percentage of white guards and Black and Brown prisoners in Elmira and Southport exceeded that of the New York State prison system as a whole: in 2008, 78.6 percent of all New York State correction officers were white men. That number climbed slightly to 83.7 percent, if you include white women. In sharp contrast, only 10.9 percent of correction officers in New York State were Black.[38] This racial pattern shifts based on geography: prisons closer to New York City, such as the infamous Sing Sing Correctional Facility, have a majority of Black and Latino/a/x guards.

The story of how a mostly white male working class in Elmira, New York, became recruited for work in an expanded prison system is both a part of a national pattern of racial division and a reflection of regional patterns of racialization in New York State. Cedric Robinson writes that in a system of racial capitalism, the "tendency within European Civilizations was thus not to homogenize but to differentiate, to exaggerate regional, cultural, and dialectical differences into 'racial ones.'"[39] In his deeply anthropological work, Robinson reminds us that there are no "neat" racializations; how people live in, resist, and shape hierarchies is very human and therefore very messy. Racial capitalism, then, requires us to understand how whiteness and Blackness as seemingly intractable patterns of human experience emerge through the structures of capitalism. Robinson's exhortation that we understand how regional differences become exaggerated into racial differences takes particular importance in the urban/rural divides that have dominated prisons, particularly as distance from home has been consistently used as a part of the punishment of incarceration.[40] He reminds us that violence and terror meted out against Black and Brown people is at the heart of maintaining a ruling elite both in the United States and globally. More specifically, as the structures of Fordism fell, the carceral state has expanded through the architecture of historical racial divisions. The expansion of the carceral state, in a process most often referred to as mass incarceration, maintains Fordism's labor hierarchies in a retooled racialization, differentiating the jailer and the jailed. Through the frame of racial capitalism, I ask: How did the arrangements of race and labor shift in New York State after deindustrialization and during prison expansion, and how are these shifts experienced, created, or recreated today by prison guards in Elmira?

Building on W.E.B. Du Bois's notion that white workers have been compensated by a "psychological wage" of white supremacy, David Roediger's *The Wages of Whiteness* ushered in a new critical approach to whiteness that followed in the footsteps of the Black radical tradition.[41] In *The Wages of Whiteness*, Roediger foregrounds the white working class's complicity in the project of racial terror. As he and other critical scholars argue, ordinary people consistently align themselves with whiteness. White workers, again and again, choose the solidarity of whiteness over alliances with Black and Brown people and even poor whites. In this vein, taking an ethnographic approach to studying a prison town and focusing on prison workers and their families, this book is a rumination on whiteness, culpability, and labor.

Maintaining the deeply disordered inequalities of racial capitalism requires tremendous violence inflicted on the poor and working classes.[42] Using the case of Elmira, I describe how Du Bois's "psychological wage" also becomes a part of the built environment of the land, a part of the infrastructure of the city, where it produces real wages and real shifts in access to wealth and power—albeit in a limited way. One of the guiding themes of this book is that the expansion of prisons into Elmira and the employment of a nearly entirely white labor force in those institutions is a part of a collective racial formation of whiteness as both a structure and a process of quotidian construction of advantage, surveillance, and policing. The expansion of the carceral state—in this case, the construction of a second prison in a small predominantly white city during the crisis of deindustrialization—was built on the racialized labor segmentation and, at the same time, has reified the categories through the construction of the categories of jailer and jailed. Race, here, should be understood as a category of difference built on political economy and simultaneously recreated through the structures created by the political economy. That is to say, to be white is a biological fiction; but to have European ancestry and be legally assigned preferential treatment by the state that allowed the growth of some limited wealth and freedoms, is real and measurable. The sediment of this history is carried into the ECF by its employees and those incarcerated there. As a category of difference, race is both a thing and a materiality created through the everyday acts of state-making, living, working, and policing one another. But, of course, being a prison guard or not is not the primary formulation of whiteness. Whiteness—even though it is a fractured experience that poor, disabled, and/or queer whites experience with extremely limited advantages—is a collective experience, a collective property, and a collective preferential relationship to the state. In this book, I show how New York State prisons are one node of the maintenance of whiteness, where the end result is some people free and others behind bars and where the median wealth of white households is now ten times that of Black households and roughly six to eight times that of Latino/a/x households.[43]

Centering the production of racial differences through labor and alienation from the ability to labor, I analyze prisons as a force in the production of racial difference in the labor market. Returning again to

Gilmore's question of what prisons do, I find that, in the case of Elmira, they immobilize one group—mostly Black and Latino/a/x men from cities throughout New York State—and they increase the political-economic power of a small group of white men who work as correction officers. This small group of workers gains a racial attachment to the state in their role as "the good guys"—the guys on the right side of the bars and on good terms with the state, the guys who are NOT criminals. If the arrival of the prison creates benefits at all, such benefits are confined to just two small groups: the local elite and, to a lesser extent, prison guards. But a prison town's losses are manifold, as the city and a growing number of residents remain poor and a sector of the working class is racialized and unjustly policed. For these reasons, the prison town must be understood in the larger context of race and class formations of whiteness.

Prison Townie

I came to this project of researching and writing about prisons as a prison "townie." Following my dad's career in the Navy, my family returned to Elmira in 1989, when I was beginning my first year of high school. I lived there until 1993, when I left for college, and I often returned until my parents retired and moved elsewhere. Prison work has been a major part not only of my hometown's economy but also of my family's sustenance for generations. After returning from World War II, both my grandfathers took jobs in corrections. My mother's father, a skilled sheet metal worker and gardener, was seeking steadier work when he took a job as a guard at Greenhaven Prison and moved his family to "the country." He eventually returned to school and became an instructor with a civilian title (a distinction made between law enforcement or control roles and those designated as social service roles) teaching sheet metal to prisoners. My dad's father worked at Coxsackie Correctional Facility, in Catskill, New York, where my dad was born. Once my paternal grandfather gained enough seniority, he too returned home to Elmira with his family, taking a job at the Elmira prison. Furthermore, at the end of his career, my grandfather's brother served as the deputy warden at the Auburn Correctional Facility until his retirement shortly after the rebellion.[44] What I know of my grandfathers' working lives I overheard at family gatherings; one died when I was five and the other became too ill to speak before I entered high school, so I never discussed their work with either of them. The family memories of prison work and prisons are fleeting: my mother remembers childhood days spent sledding down the hill in front of the ECF and recalls that her father, then a civilian worker, crossed the picket line in the correction officers' strike of 1972. I remember school functions at the Reformatory Clubhouse—a social space for prison guards and their families—and a tense day at school when at least one of my classmates' fathers was inside Southport Correctional Facility during the 1991 uprising. In my recollections of family conversations, prison work was regarded as "tough work" that was done for the purposes of steady income, but it was work that eventually compromised my grandfathers' health. At a family funeral in the summer of 2023, my aunt brought an archive from the attic to share with me. It included one grandfather's scored civil service tests for custodial officer from April and July 1952 and a weathered blue, legal-size leger where my grandfather had logged his analysis of hundreds of prisoners who might be trained in the prison sheet metal shop. With these many connections, life in Elmira, particularly white working-class and middle-income life, is as familiar as the air I breathe, evident in the nasal lilt of my own "Upstate" accent that returns summarily whenever I set foot in Chemung County.

I became interested in understanding my family's and my hometown's relationship to the prisons after becoming radicalized as a young person organizing alongside/in support of the Union of the Homeless and the Kensington Welfare Rights Union in Philadelphia, when I lived there in the late 1990s. My move to New York City in 2002 marked this shift for me. I had noticed for some time that when I introduced myself to Black and Puerto Rican New Yorkers, people from New York City, or, sometimes, anyone who had watched *Law and Order*, people would look at me sideways when I said that I was from Elmira. "Ohhhh, I know Elmira. That's where that prison is," they would reply.

In 1996, this connection was made more intimate for me when I met Ron Casanova, a long-time Black Puerto Rican housing activist and then president of the Philadelphia Union of the Homeless. As he details in his 2001 book about his lifelong activism and his involvement in the Tompkins Square Park protests, *Each One Teach One: Up and Out of Poverty,*

Memoirs of a Street Activist, Casanova was "sent Upstate" when he was a foster child. Elmira was seared in his memory as a place where white guards used hoses on boys in their cells when they were judged to be unruly.[45] Moving in the circles of poor people's organizing, I got closer to what it meant to be incarcerated and was able to make the link between poverty, racism, capitalism, and incarceration. The leadership of poor people's organizations schooled me; they taught me about myself.

The Research Process

The research for this book was conducted in starts and stops between 2008 and 2021. I began interviewing prison guards and Elmirans who had incarcerated kin in 2007. Over the course of the next two years, I conducted over forty interviews in Elmira. I met my initial interviewees through acquaintances who worked in social services in the city and then grew my research participants through their connections. From fall 2007 to summer 2008, I lived in my parents' home on Elmira's Westside, a tonier, middle-income residential neighborhood where I had also lived during high school from 1989 to 1993. The Westside of Elmira is a separately incorporated town in Chemung County (the Town of Elmira, as opposed to the City of Elmira), with separate services, such as a fire house, police force, and (lack of) civic garbage pickup. Following local narration, I consider the town of Elmira to be part of the political and economic entity of Elmira. Finally, I conducted informal research with a nonprofit support group for families of incarcerated men in New York City in the spring of 2009, attending a weekly meeting. My data collection in Elmira focused on three "places of contact" between the prison and the town: public discourse about and response to crime and criminality in Elmira, prison work, and the "roadside hospitality" center at the ECF. I interviewed forty-one key interlocutors who are actors in these arenas, conducting informal follow-up research with five of my interviewees. I completed numerous hours of observation at public forums such as city council and citizens groups meetings. In addition, I followed the work of a small nonprofit group that runs the hospitality center.

In the last ten years, I have done archival research at the Chemung County Historical Society and in the New York State Archives in Albany, New York. I have benefited from the expanded online access to newspaper archives and historical documents from Elmira City government, the New York State Department of Correctional Services, and other sources that allow me to put the current situation in broader historical context.

While most persons in this book are identified with pseudonyms, public officials are referred to using their real names. In some cases, research participants appear as an amalgamation of one or more persons.

While I may be thought of as a "native" anthropologist, in some respects it is preferable, as Narayan asserts, to redraw a messy boundary between "insider" and "outsider" and "view each anthropologist in terms of shifting identifications amid a field of interpenetrating communities and power relations."[46] In this vein, I may have been marked as an outsider in Elmira in a few aspects: my advanced education, my years in the larger cities of Philadelphia and New York, and my choice, ultimately, to leave Elmira and not to return to live there. Entering the masculine world of correction officers and prison workers, and to a lesser extent local politics, as a young-ish (well, when I started), visibly pregnant white woman may have marked me as outsider. These attributes were also perhaps a foundation for access. A few of my research participants were older white men, and they often agreed to be interviewed saying they wanted to "help me with school" or identifying with their own adult children who were also in school. Although I had made acquaintance with only two of my interlocutors before my research began, many people knew my parents, aunts and uncles, or relatives in my grandparents' generation. I was routinely asked, "Which Morrells are you related to?"—a question that requires three generations of genealogy to answer sufficiently. Finally, while my interest in the topic was spurred by my family's history and ties to the prison, none of the data presented here comes from my family or their immediate experiences. However, my family's history in the city, my years of Catholic schooling, and my grandparents' work in the prisons laid a foundation for ethnographic work on a potentially difficult topic.

As already noted, Elmira experienced a serious economic downturn in the early 1980s. During my loosely structured interviews with correction officers, I determined that it was during this period that many of my interlocutors took the civil service exam to enter this profession. I should also note that, considering that Elmira has been a prison town since the Civil War, my research demonstrated how ideas about criminality have changed over time. For example, the ECF and Southport Correctional Facility have always held a high concentration of prisoners from New York City. However, the racialized characterization and pathologizing of these prisoners has changed: in the 1950s, special logs were kept of the crimes and sentences of Italian and Italian American prisoners, allowing officials to study an ethnic group the state deemed "deviant" during that period.

Participant observation at local forums regarding public safety and news and social life more generally were key to my analysis of Elmira as a prison town. During my fieldwork, I documented a local panic about race and crime wherein many people made a connection between the rise in crime in Elmira and the two state prisons. When I spoke in Elmira about my research, noting that my topic was roughly about the relationship between the prison and the town, many people replied, "Oh, well, they're [the prisons] good for the jobs and bad because their families [the families of prisoners] move here." Others asked inquisitively about my analysis of the prison—Is it good, or is it bad? In my research and in my writing, I have paid particular attention to the attitudes of prison guards regarding race and crime and how those attitudes are and are not reflected among townspeople of different groupings. Through participant observation with a community group that runs the visitors' center at the ECF, I observed an organization of people making a different set of connections with prisoners' families. They are a liberal-minded, multiracial group of local church and synagogue members and often struggle to explain themselves to prospective volunteers. Members often consider themselves a "buffer" in difficult interactions between prison guards and families of incarcerated men. As they run the first stop of the journey on an overnight bus ride from New York City and the long walk up the steps to the prison, volunteers explain the rules of the institution, serve snacks, and drive disabled visitors to the top of the hill. Volunteers play a complicated role as both partial extensions of the authority of the prison and advocates for prisoners' families, all while helping to facilitate the social reproduction of important family relationships across a great distance. In forty-one open-ended interviews with a cross-section of Elmirans, I elicited information on the following topics: accepting or avoiding prison work, the well-being (including economic and safety concerns) and future of Elmira, the effects of prison work on social or domestic life, and the effects more prison jobs might have on community and class relations. In interviews with prison workers and their families and local civil servants, I explored social attitudes and narratives about the advantages and difficulties of prison work as a solution to unemployment. Twelve of my interviews were with prison workers, the largest number of whom were correction officers (eight) but also included counselors (two) and other civilian workers (two). Five interlocutors were formerly incarcerated men (two) or wives (two) or sisters (one) of men currently incarcerated. I conducted ten interviews with individuals involved in local politics and business, including a district attorney, a public defender, a city planner, union, civil rights, and church leaders and activists (twelve), and local business owners (two). The additional interviews were with citizens who volunteered at the prison, who lived near the prison, or whose children were interested in working at the prison (ten). Ethnographic work in and around prisons requires a particularly delicate balance. In my own work, I chose not to do ethnographic work inside the prison because of the bureaucratic requirements of the Department of Correctional Services (DOCS). For example, after an approval process in the state capital, DOCS would have had access to my field notes and would have had the opportunity to vet my work before it was published. For this reason and others, my field of study remained the city of Elmira and its various and varying relationships to the prison.

Outline of Chapters

Each of the chapters in this book makes a specific argument about the uses of Elmira as a prison town. In chapter 1, I describe the formation and reformation of Elmira's working class. To frame my argument about the particularities of whiteness as central to the formation of the carceral state, it was necessary to elucidate both Jim Crow Elmira before the migrations from Europe of the early twentieth century and the subsequent migration of Jamaican workers during World War II and their postwar deportation back to the British Empire. I look specifically at the working lives of workers at the Remington Rand typewriter factory in order to argue that the Fordist organization of work was a racialized

one, which laid the foundation for the new formations of racial capitalism in the deindustrializing period: mass incarceration.

In 1985, following the worst manufacturing job losses, Elmira's governing class accepted without question that a new prison was good for
the city of Elmira. But where did the plan for prison expansion come
from? Whose plans for Elmira were they? In chapter 2, I take on an idea
that I often heard from prison reformers in New York City—that people
Upstate *wanted prisons*. I complicate this idea by looking at how prisons as labor policy was developed in Washington DC and Albany and
made possible by Wall Street. While many Elmirans already embedded
in prison work welcomed prison expansion, this chapter focuses on how
the proposal for prison expansion emerged through state mechanisms at
the local, state, and national scale and intertwined with the interests of
capital. A new prison was sold to Elmira's leaders as a source of jobs in
a period of high unemployment. But what kind of work is prison work?
Chapter 3 is built on interviews with prison guards that highlight prison
work as a middle-class job that trades in other forms of stigma. I build on
theorizations of whiteness as crucial to the construction of class identity
in the United States to argue that prison work is work valued solely for
income and access and eschewed as a life vocation.

According to Elmirans, the stigma of prison work is not the only problem that prison brings. In Chapter 4, I outline a panic that emerged in
Elmira, as its citizens attempted to trace increases in crime to the families of men incarcerated in the town; I trace the origins of this panic to
the racial orderings created by the carceral state—one of the ways the
prison is a porous place. Continuing with the theme of the porousness
of the prison, Chapter 5 weaves together scenes from domestic violence
survivors, the COVID pandemic, and Elmira's courtrooms in order to
show how the prison and town are intricately connected social envi-
ronments. Chapter 6 builds on this argument through an ethnography
of the visitor's center at the ECF.

In the final chapter I argue for an abolitionist decarceration grounded
in the needs of both prisoners and people in prison towns and the places
they love and call home. In the end, I argue that the data from this book
shows that prisons are sources of an uneven immiseration on both sides
of the bars.

1   Deindustrialization, Racialized Labor, and Prison Expansion

In 1944, James O'Connor of Kingston, Jamaica, then a colony of the United Kingdom, came to Elmira to work in iron production at General Electric's (GE) Elmira Foundry. James was one of 111 Jamaican men recruited by GE from across the Caribbean and Latin America to fill what GE said were one thousand open jobs in the foundry, in the context of World War II labor shortages. In Jamaica, James had worked for ten years at a cricket club. On his first day in Elmira, he spoke to the local newspaper and was outfitted with new steel-toed boots for the dangerous work at the foundry. He and Eustace Fothergill, another man in the group, ate stewed beef, mashed potatoes, and rice prepared in a communal kitchen in their barracks on the foundry's campus. James and his coworkers did "heavy and dangerous" aspects of the work, such as "pouring of metal and operating the annealing oven," making gray iron castings for GE trucks, tanks, ships, and aircraft engines.[1] Unlike immigrant men from Italy and Poland recruited to work in Elmira's industries in the early twentieth century, James was likely deported to Jamaica after completing the length of the contract on April 28, 1946.[2]

A generation later, before the onset of the economic downturn of the 1980s, Roy Mayers, a white American-born man, was working in a warehouse and decided to take the civil service test to become a correction officer. When I interviewed Roy in 2008, he told me, "We knew that that was a more secure employment than where we were at. Even if the plant was still there and going great guns, a state job would have been better time off, better benefits. There's no doubt there." But after being offered the job, Roy considered not becoming a prison guard:

We were making ends meet, the lifestyle wasn't too bad, my wife was working at the time. One day I was in the [warehouse]. . . . I put the forklift in reverse and I'm ready to back out in reverse and [a supervisor] was right behind me. And he says, "Roy, I gotta ask you a question. There's a rumor going around that you're going to turn that job down with the state." And I said, "I been toyin' with the idea, yeah, I thought about it." He says, "Let me tell you one thing. If you do, I'm gonna kick your ass all the way around this warehouse." He said, "You're the only one who passed the written test, who passed the physical test. If you turn this down, I'm gonna kick your ass all over this warehouse." He says, "Git outta here."

Roy took the correction officer job, and the warehouse where he had worked closed a few years later.

In this chapter, I tell the story of Elmira's racialized working class beginning in the Fordist period, through the collapse and restructuring of industrial manufacturing and industrial unionism, to the city elites' and their allies' attempt at a *carceral reindustrialization* in the late 1980s. The story of New York's expanding carceral state is the story of how whiteness and Blackness emerge, reemerge, and are strengthened through the categories of work. I argue that in order for us to understand the racialized system within the prison—where a majority Black and Latino/a/x prisoner population is guarded by overwhelmingly white guards, a situation common across the state—we must understand the racialized history of labor in Elmira in the context of New York State and the world. In other words, it isn't just a fact of nature that prison of mostly Black and Brown men is controlled and surveilled by mostly white guards; rather, the racialized history of labor set the stage for the current pattern. While both James and Roy represent Elmira's working class, albeit in different ways, it was the experience of men like Roy of European ancestry whose working lives were meant to be "saved" by an attempt at a carceral reindustrialization.[3]

These two men's histories also frame Elmira's racialized working class as a part of an imperial world economy in the twentieth century. While these are relatively small populations—James representing a few hundred Jamaican men who did industrial work on temporary work visas and Roy representing a few thousand white men who became prison guards during the postindustrial period—their access to work and citizenship reflect how the enforcement of borders have been used to fortify both the United States as an imperial power *and* the preferential citizenship of the category of white workers. The jobs available to working-class Elmirans across immigration status have shifted over the last three generations and those divisions have been lived in a racialized way. Historian of Jamaican guestworkers in the United States Cindy Hahamovitch writes that during World War II, in addition to Caribbean and Mexican workers, "Canadians came too but no one bothered to count them; they were not bound by contract and officials didn't seem to worry about whether they left. In the imagination of U.S. officials, guestworkers were men of color whose movements had to be carefully monitored."[4] The story of racialization and the maintenance of whiteness for some workers was written by borders and their enforcement.[5]

I follow the shifting formations of race and class in Elmira from three perspectives. First, I show the development of Elmira's whitened immigrant working class at the Remington Rand typewriter factory, focusing at times on the life of my great aunt. Second, I show how Jamaican workers on guest visas work in the same Remington Rand factories as their mostly white-coded coworkers during wartime production, but without the access to U.S. citizenship. Finally, I look at a series of obituaries for Remington Rand employees to show how Elmirans navigated the dissolution of the Fordist system of labor and how people across the city imagined its future. Rather than separate from the development of the carceral state, the creation of distinct racializations in the categories of work and citizenship was pivotal in the imagination of who belongs behind bars and who would walk the concrete floors securing their incarceration.

Fordism's Wake

The period of near-full employment during World War II and the years of relative working-class affluence during the twenty-five or so years after are recalled as the glory days of the City of Elmira. At the dawn of the twentieth century, Elmira transformed from a small regional trading post—a railroad stop—into an industrial center, home to several international companies, including Remington Rand (bought by Sperry and now part of Unisys), U.S. Steel's American Bridge Works, and Bendix (now Honeywell). These corporations grew and so did the population of the city, as tens of thousands of people—many of them European immigrants—sought to work in the burgeoning steel industry. During World War II and the postwar period, workers won access to health insurance, were offered housing or housing assistance, and, often, secured career-long work in manufacturing. All of this was achieved through robust and rapid unionization and union militancy. In contrast to the prisons, which people repeatedly told me during my fieldwork were "just there," seemingly natural parts of the Elmira landscape, the steel-based industries are remembered as places where people were proud to work.

But the good times would not last. In the waning days of the manufacturing boom, prisons began to emerge across the country as what Ruth Wilson Gilmore has called a "geographical solution that purports to solve social problems by repeatedly removing people from disordered, deindustrialized milieus and depositing them somewhere else."[6] Thus, when Southport Correctional Facility was built in Elmira in 1988, it was lauded by its proponents less for its purported role in the state's public safety than for the jobs it created. The expansion of the carceral state must therefore be analyzed as a process equally political and economic, one that involved building infrastructures, hiring Upstate labor and disempowering downstate and labor, transferring money from state coffers to the infrastructures of punishment. This process occurred parallel to and dialectically with the disappearance of the higher wages for some workers in the post-Fordist period. The crises of post-Fordism—of revenue loss, of wealth redistribution, and of profound loss of income, employment, and stability—emerged through the same racialized mechanisms that supported its development.[7] Despite the breakdown of Fordism, the specter of a Fordist past remained, and remains, critical to understanding what was expected to replace it. In Elmira, the white male workers who made up the bulk of the well-paid working class were expected to be the new recruits to prison work; they were construed by the city's mayor as men who didn't want to receive "municipal welfare" but were in search of "good" work.[8]

In their work on post-Fordism in Italy, Muehlebach and Shoshan argue that the memories of Fordism "continue to bring forth powerful affective attachments," particularly "the promise of relative economic security and well-being, plausible middle-class aspirations" that existed for some workers.[9] In other words, because Fordism meant (for an unevenly advantaged group of workers) access to relative stability, the endurance of their affections for that time period is not entirely surprising. The ghosts of Fordism give an architecture, however unstable, to the hopes, dreams, and expectations of many working-class New Yorkers, as well as those of the governments that structure their futures. However, a key characteristic of the Fordist period was the division of the working class into a protected class of "skilled workers" with stable labor contracts and a more precarious group of people left outside of this deal, often on racial lines.[10] As historian Laura Renata Martin writes, "Fordism was not just about a particular relationship between labor and capital, but about the relationships and divisions between working-class people themselves."[11] In the post-Fordist state, these racialized divisions are fortified through the expansion of the carceral state that immobilizes largely Black and Latino/a/x men from the workplace through their incarceration and surveillance while employing more white men as guards with a preferential relationship to the state.[12]

In my analysis of guard labor, I do not intend to diminish the prison as a place of confinement, dispossession, and loss for incarcerated men and women. Rather, I seek to shift the focus of Elmira's labor history outside of the factory onto the carceral state. The prison is itself a site of extractive value and productive of racial differences in order to facilitate other forms of dispossession. At the end of the chapter, I outline how racial divisions of labor were intensified in the postindustrial period through the rapid and massive use of criminalization and incarceration.

As the Northeast deindustrialized, Elmira became a classic American Rust Belt city. Over the course of sixty-plus years marked by waves of manufacturing job losses, more than one-third of the population of Elmira has moved elsewhere, the city shrinking from 49,716 people in 1950 to 26,523 residents in 2020.[13] Working-class neighborhoods have become poor neighborhoods, churches have lost members and have been forced to consolidate with other churches, and, as in many poor places, young people with college degrees now leave the area in search of work in bigger cities. But to understand how the labor market shifted into one where prisons became a more significant aspect of the economy, we must first examine how the landscape of work, wages, and job loss in a racialized Fordist economy structured the experiences of working-class Elmirans and New Yorkers in the 1930s to the 1970s. I highlight the experiences of workers at two of Elmira's major factories during this period: the Remington Rand typewriter plant on Elmira's Southside (where my father's aunt Margaret Smykowski worked for her entire career), which closed in 1972, and the Elmira Foundry, which recruited workers from Jamaica between 1944 and 1946. I show how these factories organized social, political, and economic life in Elmira, and I describe the experiences of a small number of workers who made the transition to prison work from manufacturing work while many others were left with no prospects.

"Any Other Remington Rand Families Remember This?"

Remington Rand was an international leader in typewriter manufacturing. The Elmira plant operated from 1936–1972, employing tens of thousands of townspeople over the decades. The eighty-three acres of property, three-quarters of which are in Elmira and the remainder in Southport, lie adjacent to the Consolidated Rail Corporation, formerly the Erie-Lackawanna Railroad.[14]

My father's maternal aunt Margaret Smykowski worked at the factory for many years following World War II. Her parents and older siblings had migrated in the late nineteenth century from Bohemia in central Europe and settled in rural northern Pennsylvania. My father's mother and Margaret grew up on a farm there; the sisters moved to Elmira for work in the 1930s. Margaret got a job at Remington Rand, married, and continued to work at the factory until her retirement. She was even eulogized in the *Elmira Star-Gazette* as "MK Smykowski, Rand Retiree," as was common at the time.[15] For at least a short time, she was the District 58 International Association of Machinists' recording secretary and was a member of the Ladies Auxiliary Union Social Club in the late 1940s. Her husband, Stanley, worked at Bendix Electronics, an automotive manufacturer. Their factory jobs allowed them to buy a small house in

Elmira and gave them access to health care and ample free time: Margaret became a champion bowler, volunteered at church, and crocheted baby blankets for her friends and family. She saved enough money to leave my family a small inheritance when she passed away in 1999. Their work was union work, which meant job protections, regular contractual wage increases, and the possibility to have an advocate speak on their behalf if a grievance arose.

This story of the factories of Elmira and the working-class people who worked in them might seem like just a "local" story, but the process of class formation is never geographically disconnected from working people's role in production in a global capitalist economy. At the height of Remington Rand's production in 1946, Margaret was one of sixty-five hundred people employed at the Elmira plant. From 1936 to 1972, Elmira's workers made every typewriter produced under the Remington Rand name, which held the industry standard. Through these typewriters, Elmirans' labor reached across the world. In the local paper in 1955, workers proudly relayed their expertise in making typewriters, noting the specifications of typewriters in Yiddish and Arabic that moved from right to left and a particular mechanical process for marking Burmese letters.[16] The company competed for contracts with workers across Europe, often vying to keep Elmira jobs from being outsourced abroad.[17]

An expansion of wartime production in the early 1940s meant a huge growth in Elmira's population. Between 1940 and 1942, nine thousand people moved to the city, a 20 percent increase. The Works Progress Administration saw Elmira as an essential wartime manufacturing hub and therefore subsidized the development of residential housing.[18] This led to the most dramatic population boom in Elmira, by now well established as a place of industrial production, with a strategic proximity to New York City and sited along the road from Chicago to the rest of the industrial corridor.

I reviewed sixty-one obituaries of workers whose families noted their work at Remington Rand in their death notices in the *Elmira Star-Gazette* from 1990–2000.[19] Most of these paid, short obituaries included a list of the individual's surviving relatives, the church congregation to which he or she belonged, and their employer or former employer. Judging by their social milieu, and from scanning the websites of churches I was unfamiliar with, I estimate that all but one of these workers was white. There were significant cultural differences within this group: men with Italian names who attended St. Anthony's Church on the Eastside, women with Irish names who attended St. Mary's on the Southside, and those with German names who attended the Protestant churches downtown and in the surrounding rural areas. While I am ultimately making an educated guess about their racial identity, what is abundantly clear in these short life stories written for posterity by their families is that there was a certain pride in their work. It was something to rely on and an identity to carry through retirement and old age; it framed the story of their life. Generally speaking, even outside these sixty-one cases, in Elmira, at Remington Rand, most of the workers who had access to this kind of better paying work were white. Importantly, it was access to well-paid work and to the relative comforts afforded to European immigrants and their descendants, or those who passed as such, that was central to the *maintenance and creation* of whiteness. In other words, the workers were granted access to whiteness through the particularities of decent wages at a union shop and the lifestyle that came with it.[20]

But the Fordist period workforce was not entirely white; instead, racial and gendered mechanisms of employment shaped a group's experience of work. Black workers were more likely to do more dangerous work, less likely to be maintained as long-term workers, less likely to be promoted to management positions, and often kept out of unions.[21] In the 1950s and '60s, Elmira remained residentially segregated, with a relatively small Black population. From 1850 to 1950, only 1 to 2 percent of the population of all of Chemung County was classified as "colored" (not white). The number rose slightly, to 2 to 4 percent, from 1936 to 1972 during the time Remington Rand was an active plant. Since 1970 the Black population in the city of Elmira alone, where almost all Black Chemung County residents live, has doubled, from 7.9 percent to 14.9 percent of the total population in 2020.[22]

Based on my review of obituaries and the racial politics of the era, it is reasonable to assume that there were few Black workers in the factories. In an apparently exceptional case, one African American man who worked at Remington Rand building typewriters, William "Mickey" Jones, eventually became a barber instructor at the Elmira Correctional Facility while maintaining his own shop.[23] Mickey was a member of the local African Methodist Episcopal Church and a volunteer for the Northside community development agency, the Elmira Equal Opportunity Program. I did a similar review of obituaries, also in the *Star-Gazette*, of congregants at the longest-serving African American church in Elmira, the Frederick Douglass AME Zion Church. While some of these obituaries did not include the decedent's place of work, I did find here the stories of a female nurse's aide and two female hospital employees; a man who had retired from American Bridge (a subsidiary of U.S. Steel); another from General Electric; and two from the Department of Corrections chaplaincy. For example, in the obituary of Ira Mae Dumas, her daughter stated, "My mother was . . . ahead of her time. Although she was relegated to mundane work, being a nurse aide at Arnot Ogden and St. Joe's, she wasn't frustrated. It didn't stop her from exploring the future."[24] This mention of being "relegated to mundane work" reflects the experiences of many Black workers in terms of what work was accessible to them. As Tom Sugrue documents for Detroit, Black workers suffered significantly in the Fordist period, and any gains in wealth, access to leisure, and higher tiers of work were eroded by deindustrialization.[25]

The Factory and Working-Class Life

It is difficult to overestimate the centrality of Remington Rand and other manufacturers to working-class life in Elmira. Throughout World War II, a rifle league boasted six teams of Remington Rand workers who competed with other teams of workers from the Elmira Reformatory, Sears, and the Elmira Foundry (which would later become American Bridge Works). Throughout the 1940s, there was a large and active city softball league, including two industrial leagues, which each included a team from Remington Rand. There was also a church league, which included the Irish church (St. Patrick's), the Italian church (St. Anthony's), the Frederick Douglass AME church, two white Methodist churches, and one white Presbyterian church. There were also many social clubs based around work, which were central to the social life of the city. When the factories left, people not only had less access to decent wages but also struggled to make and maintain the community ties that had been formed at recreational softball and bowling leagues outside of work.

In late April 2020, as I was finishing this chapter, a woman posted a faded picture of ten men in "Remington Rand Hitting Machines" T-shirts to a Facebook group I belong to called "If You're Really from the Elmira, NY Area." She and a friend guessed that this photo of the Remington Rand softball team, of which her father was a member, was taken sometime in the late 1940s or 1950s. A month before, she had posted a picture of a tote bag with the phrase "The Sassy One from Remington" and a picture of an anthropomorphized cat leaning on a bowling ball bag and a company notebook to be used for typewriting practice. On her post, she asked, "Any other Remington Rand families remember this?" Other members of the group recalled the Remington typewriter notebooks and said they too had saved a few of them. I was struck that nearly fifty years after the closure of Elmira's Remington Rand plant, the social experiences of those who had worked together there remained a point of nostalgia and a meaningful part of their identity.[26] For these women, and to some degree for me, remembering the work in the factories is a part of a shared understanding of what it means to be "from Elmira." It is not news that many people form deep relationships at work. What is interesting, in this case, is how the experience of working alongside one another in a factory was paired with a rich social world, in which workers socialized as representatives of their factories outside of work. The softball team was just one of many organized activities: the plant housed five bowling lanes and hosted basketball and bowling teams. In 1952 ten thousand people attended the company picnic at the local amusement center, Harris Hill.

When the factories departed, they left a huge void in the social lives and bank accounts of many working-class Elmirans. When the town's boosters proposed to welcome one of the state's planned prisons in order to lure jobs to the area, it was this era, this organization of life, this "fragile affluence" that many people in town imagined could be recreated.[27]

From Jamaica to the GE Foundry in Elmira

U.S. entry into World War II bolstered this alignment of relative abundance and whiteness while also opening new uneven paths to immigrant workers. Seeking to expand their pool of workers, in 1944, representatives of General Electric Company sought to recruit workers in Barbados to work in the Elmira Foundry, but the Barbadian colonial government prohibited workers from migrating because their labor was needed for the sugar cane harvest. Still, during the war, twelve thousand Jamaicans and twenty thousand workers total from across the Caribbean came to the United States to do seasonal agricultural work and to work in the factories.[28] In September 1944, 111 Jamaican men arrived in Elmira to begin work at the Elmira Foundry.

In Hahamovitch's history of Jamaican guestworkers in the United States, Jamaicans were to be sent to the U.S. North, as unlike Bahamians, they would "chafe" at the "system of formal segregation" in the South.[29] She writes, "The Jamaican guestworkers who came to the United States during World War II were in fact an unusually worldly, educated, and articulate group of farmworkers. Most probably came to the United States . . . desperate for economic opportunities that were unavailable to them in Jamaica, but they were also imbued with the knowledge that they were war workers, sent by an allied country to do an essential job. Determined to be treated as the equals of whites, they boldly defied growers' expectations that they would be cheap, tractable, and submissive."[30] Reflecting my own reading of newspapers and archives in Elmira, Hahamovitch's narrative of this period suggests that white Americans in the north were more welcoming to the Black Caribbean workers than they were to Black American workers, and the local (white) press were eager to make comparisons between the two groups.

Along with workers from Mexico and Puerto Rico, workers from Barbados, Jamaica, and Honduras were recruited as temporary, seasonal workers.[31] Unlike the immigrant workers of previous generations, they were not granted access to citizenship. One of these men was James O'Connor, whose migration story opened this chapter. By spending time here focusing on a small number of Jamaican workers whose labor supported the war effort, I build on the literature that makes the connection between access to citizenship and the whitening of European populations who previously had not been considered white and the second-class status that befell migrant workers from Mexico, Puerto Rico, and, in this case, Jamaica. Doing so highlights an important way that the racial hierarchies of Elmira, on which the carceral state apparatuses would be built, emerged.

FIG. 1. Eustace Fothergill and James O'Connor, two men recruited from Jamaica on temporary work visas for wartime production, serve helpings of stewed beef in the barracks of the Elmira Foundry, where they lived and worked. *Elmira Star-Gazette*, September 26, 1944, A7. Star-Gazette—USA TODAY NETWORK.

During their time in Elmira, the Jamaican workers lived in separate "worker's quarters" on the campus of Remington Rand, with their own cook whom they had brought with them. They worshipped at the Black churches of Elmira and gave presentations on Jamaican life to the congregations. They received packages of cigarettes from home and purchased new steel-toed boots. At an event billed as "Life in Modern Jamaica," presented to the Young People's Group of the First Congregational Church in the nearby city of Binghamton, a group of workers served a dinner of curried chicken and mango juice. Like the case of the Bracero workers from Mexico, the labor contracts between Jamaica and the United States were significant for their recruitment of workers to the United States between 1921 and the passage of the Hart-Celler Act in 1965—when other forms of legal migration were otherwise restricted. The War Manpower Commission had hired the workers on temporary visas; after their work contracts were over, they would be sent home. In Jamaica, the men had worked at cricket clubs and as mechanics, painters, and truck drivers; now, they had been recruited to do "unskilled labor" in the United States.[32]

But their bosses resisted letting them go at the end of their contracts: they had learned their tasks and were now sought after as skilled labor. On at least one occasion in 1945, there were reports that Jamaican workers in Elmira were doing "extra employment," or working outside of their contracts, which was regarded as "taking" work from American workers. They were reported to the War Manpower Commission, Walter J. O'Neill, the local area director of the commission, told the newspapers, and if workers were found in violation of their specific contract of work—only at the foundry—they could be deported. This protectionism was supported by the commission and served both to isolate and racialize the workers by limiting their ability to work and to earn.[33]

Despite such efforts to divide workers, at least one local union welcomed the Jamaicans: United Electrical, Radio, and Machine Workers Local 310 of the CIO. The Jamaican workers participated in a two-month strike in January and February of 1946, just months before their contract to work at the foundry would end. This does not necessarily mean that the union fought against the racialization of the era, and it is possible that the Jamaican workers were included in the collective bargaining union strategically, to prevent them from being strike breakers. Nonetheless, the success of the strike brought a $2 per day wage increase for all the workers, including the Jamaican men who lived and worked at the foundry.

While very little has been written about these workers in Elmira, or anywhere else in the United States for that matter, at least a dozen of the men returned home to Jamaica and then came back to Elmira on different visas, to work at the General Electric foundry. Charles Brown lived his adult life in Elmira after coming to the city to work at the foundry during the war. In 1993 Charles Brown lent his naturalization papers and a hand-drawn map of Jamaica to a local exhibit at the Chemung County Historical Society.[34]

Black Caribbean, Black New York

From the moment of their entry into New York harbor, the press mused about the Jamaicans' place in America's racial hierarchy. The men were described as follows: "Splendidly polite, with a British graciousness, these soft-spoken Jamaicans dress no differently from their North American neighbors. They have a gentle, quick-spoken accent of their own, with a British touch. If they speak rapidly, it is difficult at first to understand them, but speaking slowly, they are able to be understood."[35] In another instance the workers were referred to as "Negro" workers from the Caribbean, highlighting the clear categorization of Black workers from the Caribbean into the American racial hierarchies.[36]

Federal immigration programs—dictated by the needs of corporations like Remington Rand—determined which workers were eligible to become American and who had the right to be brought fully into well-paid working-class jobs in Elmira and cities like it across the country. A broader look at the labor history of a specific place can help us understand the historical development of the racial categorization of crime and criminal justice and how the enforcement of borders in work have contributed to the making of the carceral state. As Elmira enters the period of deindustrialization, who is deemed eligible, deserving, and necessary to need "good" work has been shaped by historical patterns of inclusion and exclusion.

"Elmira's Remington Rand Is Dead"

In 1972 the Remington Rand factory closed its doors in Elmira. While some production had moved to Europe in 1961, layoffs in the hundreds followed a brutal strike in 1969, leaving only seventeen hundred jobs in Elmira. Remington Rand wasn't the only case: Bendix Electronics, which had made bicycle brakes at their Elmira plant since 1901, moved production to Mexico; Smith Corona moved to England. These industries shifted to flexible models of production and sought out capitalist countries keen on the privatization of public goods. In the United States, cutbacks to education meant schools weren't buying typewriters, and plant management wasn't maintaining the new manufacturing technologies to compete with other producers. In 1972 the final 690 Remington Rand workers were laid off and the production of the last typewriters was sent to a plant in Toronto. The local paper's Remington Rand closure coverage began with, "Elmira's Remington Rand is dead, a 37-year-old casualty of economics."[37]

The newspaper highlighted the experiences of laid-off workers. There were the familiar narratives of deindustrialization: one man had worked at the plant since he was eighteen and had never done any other paid work; older workers found it hard to get work other places; couples who had long had two incomes from Rand were doubly screwed. The questions from the interviewers at the time are still familiar to us now: Did workers have mortgages to pay, college tuitions to account for?[38] This narrative of loss has been a well-documented aspect of deindustrialization.

While many people blamed the unions for companies' departures, some of Rand's laid-off workers had their own analysis. Workers interviewed at the time attributed the factory's competitive weakness to the lack of import taxes on products made outside the United States. Albert Baccille, who worked as a straighter at Rand for twenty-five years, noted that "what people are asking for [money-wise] won't make as much difference as the policies controlling import-export proportions." Baccille thought the recent strike and meager wage increases sought by workers weren't a significant loss for the company; rather, he the increasing globalization of the labor market was the likely force behind the closure.[39]

In this small city losing thousands of jobs, everyone would know some-one struggling with unemployment, but at least to the press, receiving public assistance was taboo. A few laid-off workers vowed never to apply for welfare, one man noting that he would rather "dig a ditch" first; this worker also noted that no one appeared to be hiring to do that work, either. But the Department of Public Welfare's deputy commissioner noted that so much job loss meant that he was deeply worried about funding the necessary social services for laid off workers; at the same time, he was unable to make a direct connection between new appli-cations for public assistance and the plant closures for lack of data.[40]

From Deindustrialization to Prison Expansion

Deindustrialization upset the fragile affluence that some workers, includ-ing workers at Rand and Bendix Electronics, had gained in the postwar period. I argue in this book that the growth of prisons was imagined as an antidote to this time of loss, and more particularly, that the racialized landscape of labor during this time set the groundwork for the growth of the prisons in many places, including Elmira. How working people imagined their safety, how people imagined their future of work, was born out of the wins and contradictions of the postwar period.

As was common practice at the time for most stories of local interest, the home addresses of twenty-three laid-off workers were printed in the newspaper. I plotted the addresses on a map and noted that the two dozen workers interviewed in the article lived within a six-mile radius of the plant on the Southside of Elmira, with the majority clustered around the plant. It is not surprising, of course, that people like to live near their places of work. What is notable is how the Southside of Elmira and the village of Southport now reflect this loss. Gordon Gaughan, a guard I spoke with in 2008, lamented the decline of his neighborhood: "A lot of people who lived on the Southside worked for the railroad, Remington Rand, and American LaFrance. And those people lived in that area. And [now] there's nothing left on the Southside." Southport Correctional Facility, heralded as a state investment in jobs for locals, was built less than a mile from the former Remington Rand site in 1988.

There were some efforts by remnants of the labor movement to offer an alternate vision out of the crisis by expanding unemployment monies until workers found jobs, creating a group called the Greater Elmira Unemployment Council. The council was a part of a national group that organized unemployed workers and pushed for the creation of public sector jobs. The group received support and minimal funding from local churches, specifically the office of Social Ministry of Catholic Charities. But no federal program to expand public sector work was forthcoming. Instead, New York State went the path of carceral reindustrialization, building thirty-five new prisons across the state in a matter of twenty years. In 1988 one of those new prisons was built in Elmira.

For Elmirans, including both of my grandfathers, work at the ECF offered a "middle-class job" with benefits and wages parallel to those won by unions in the postwar period. Indeed, in order to recruit workers, the prisons offered benefits similar to those they had enjoyed in the halcyon industrial days. As the factory work began to leave Elmira, coinciding with the rise of the Black Power movements and prison uprisings, the job of prison guard became professionalized. This not only increased guards' pay but also contributed to the general "professionalization" of the job of social control.

Many of the guards I spoke with had taken jobs in the prison during the boom in hiring and prison construction after 1980. Given the larger economic decline in New York and around the country, working in a prison provided stability, one that was no longer found in manufacturing. Roy Mayers, the worker whose story began this chapter, left his warehouse job in the late 1970s and spent the bulk of his working life walking the concrete floors of the ECF. A woman by the name of Blanche Sanders Luther left Remington Rand a bit earlier, in the mid-1960s, to become a correction officer. Her sister described that decision for Luther's obituary in the newspaper: "'She loved it,' said her sister Geneva Yattaw, of Elmira. "The family never tried to dissuade Mrs. Luther from this new career path," Yattaw said. 'They didn't say anything about it. It was a well-paying job and had good benefits, and that's what she liked about it.'"[41] Although it is not explicit, I sense in this obituary the idea shared with me by other correction officers that people don't understand prison work. Perhaps, as I discuss more in chapter 4, they thought it gauche, given the perceived distastefulness of being close to prisoners and the brutality of the whole prison. At the same time, they understood that the benefits could lure a person to work there.

Gordon Gaughn told me he took a job as a prison guard at the height of unemployment in Elmira.

> My degree was in sociology, and I had a minor in psychology, and I was certified to teach. But, I couldn't get a job. I spent two years substitute teaching. This was '78–'79, and I couldn't—I wasn't makin' any money. I couldn't make over $6,000 a year. So one of my friends said, "Well, why don't you take the correctional officer's test." And he said, "Well, it's going to be about twice the amount of money you're making. You'll probably make about $14,000 to start out." And I needed something financially to get myself on my feet. And I was sick and tired. I wanted a decent car, I wanted to get out on my own, and I said, "Okay, so I'll try for five years." And five years turns into ten. And then you're married with two kids, and all of a sudden (pause) then I went through the strike, and the strike really boosted our pay. 1979. Yeah, we went from $14,000 to $30,000 almost overnight. And then I said, "I'm ten years into a marriage and raising kids and the $30,000 in this area, that's quite a bit of money," so ten years turns into fifteen.

A number of the correction officers I spoke with had been hired during the construction boom under Governor Mario Cuomo, and in the mid-2000s were newly retired or on the brink of retirement. When talking about why they had taken jobs in the prison, many explained that there was little other work available to them at that time of economic crisis. Greg Shaunessy, who had worked in a factory that manufactured cardboard boxes and as a janitor prior to taking the correction officer civil service exam, recalled, "At the time when I took the guard test, it was coming off the Carter years . . . Chemung County had the highest unemployment in the state. You couldn't find a job." Over the years, he had supplemented his income as a prison guard with the family farm that his wife helped him run. He was eager to return to farm work after his retirement. Gordon Gaughan, explained it this way: "It was the '80s. There was nothing else. I had a BA in criminal justice and psychology. I was going to take it 'til something else comes along." Gordon said that many of his coworkers had college or advanced degrees, or worked in

skilled trades, "people with master's degrees, bachelor's degrees, weld-
ers. . . . Their goal in life wasn't to be a prison guard," he added, "but
once they locked into it, it's good money for the area."

The idea of steady work with good benefits as an anchor for family
life was a common theme in discussions with correction officers, and
it was also a common argument for keeping prisons open by Upstate
politicians. Rosie Conti, a local union official, put wages from prison
work in the broader perspective of the local economy: "See, when you
lose high-paying industrial jobs or a union job with good benefits, and
then you [try to] make it up in retail, I mean, it's a joke. It's minimum
wage or part time. All of these department stores are hiring a handful
of people part time . . . So it's okay if, say, your husband is a guard and
you're just filling in part-time. But if you have to live on that, like a single
income, you're gonna die." In contrast to those minimum wage retail jobs,
the average annual income of a state worker in Elmira was $60,000 in
2005, which was roughly double the average household wage in Elmira
as a whole and triple the household income of poor and working-class
neighborhoods on the Southside, Eastside, and Downtown Elmira.[42]

Many Elmirans, prison workers and others, spoke of prison work as a
"good job" because of the package of benefits that come with state work.
Still, there continues to be considerable unease in Elmira regarding the
centrality of prisons in the local economy. Faith Bell, a young white pro-
fessional who was working as part of a larger network of young people
to fight Elmira's "brain drain" and encourage young college educated
people to stay in the area, commented that, with the prisons, "there is
not value added, really, beyond the steady employment." She made the
comparison to a small, privately owned business team that might stay
anchored in the area: "Beyond providing jobs it's not like you've got the
prisons so invested. DOCS [Department of Correctional Services] isn't
invested in Elmira and [the idea] 'let's make Elmira a better place.' It's
not like, for instance, a restaurant sponsoring a baseball team. Elmira
prison isn't doing that."[43] In her assessment, a private company might
be more interested in improving Elmira than a state enterprise, which
seems to her to be less a part of the place.

When I spoke with a member of the Elmira Chamber of Commerce
asking about the prison's relationship to the larger economy, she said,

"Nobody moves to Elmira to be a correction officer. It's more like the prisons are there and there just happens to be a job there." She added, incorrectly, that the prisons are "self-contained units" and the medical facilities in Elmira are only used by prisoners in acute emergencies. She added, "Not everyone is able to do that job." Both residents were concerned with Elmira's image as a place, and both had concluded that prison work is not work that the town is or should be proud of. It is important to emphasize that carceral reindustrialization precludes other types of development, most notably gentrification and tourism, two marketing patterns of "place" that have helped other small cities succeed.[44] One local doctor who had treated inmates at St. Joseph's Hospital noted that the prison jobs were important to the area, but "the prison industry is a pretty rough industry. It's not like the tourist industry. It's not like the wineries." Prisons, adopted over the last forty years as a "solution" for Elmira's economic woes, continue to raise many questions about the meaning of Elmira as a place.

2   Who Built the Southport Correctional Facility?

In 2003, while conducting my first formal research in Elmira, I looked for "prisons" in the card catalog at the downtown Steele Memorial Library. On a small white card filed under "prisons" was typed "see also 'Economic Development.'" I wondered: Was it so simple for Elmirans that prisons were useful for economic development? What did "development" mean in this context? While a municipal historian of Elmira might write a simple "yes" to that question, as an anthropologist, I wrote a different set of questions.

In 1985, at the height of the prison construction boom in New York State, the City of Elmira threw its hat in the ring for both public monies for prisons and enterprise zone tax incentives. This is perhaps not surprising, considering that Elmira had lost thousands of manufacturing jobs in the first half of the 1980s and was in a state of crisis, with the highest unemployment rate on record in New York State. American LaFrance fire engines, Remington Rand typewriters, Ann Page Foods, American Bridge Works, and Bendix electronics factories all closed their doors. Storefronts in downtown Elmira that had not yet reopened following the flooding from Hurricane Agnes in 1972 showed no sign of recovery. In 1985 one-third of the population was living below the poverty line, and the number of Elmirans on public assistance had increased by 25 percent from 1982 to 1986.[1] True, that same year, there was a wave of hope and promise as an unused manufacturing plant reopened. The plant moved rather quickly to temporary production schedules, which meant unreliable employment for workers.[2]

In public testimony to the UDC at a 1986 hearing on State Empowerment Zones, boosters from across central New York State, including the Kennedy Valve fire hydrant plant operations manager and representatives from Conrail and the Southern Tier Regional Planning Board, pleaded for an influx of capital for the future of their cities and towns. But Vincent Tese, the head of the powerful engine of municipal financing for construction Urban Development Corporation (UDC), called for private capital, rather than federal or state grants, to revitalize the New York State economy. A report written by Tese made clear that the UDC's New York would be rebuilt by replacing manufacturing jobs with jobs in computers and biotechnology that would be lured to the state through incentives offered to businesses.[3] The rules for what would "work" in New York were proposed to apply equally to vastly different places. For example, in the first round of selecting enterprise zones to receive state funding—namely tax abatements and wage supports—to "support" private businesses, among the first ten cities chosen were Ogdensburg along the Canadian border, East Harlem in New York City, and Auburn, another prison town. Eventually three new prisons were built in Ogdensburg, which had suffered a 15 percent unemployment rate after the collapse of the mining industry.[4]

In this chapter, I offer an alternate argument to the idea that Upstate New Yorkers' desires were the primary drivers of prison expansion. Rather, I argue that the plans for the expansion of prisons originated in the centers of power in Albany and New York City and built on the historical layers and fissures of racial capitalism. It is certainly true that many Elmirans welcomed the prison, and more Elmirans didn't question the need for carceral solutions to the problems of New York State. But in order to answer the question "Who were the architects of prisons as a plan for economic development in Elmira?" this chapter leads us through the winding paths of federal, state, and municipal governments negotiating over the powers of the state to harness small amounts of capital for prison construction and maintenance. From the period 1981 to 1988, a group of local politicians and businessmen—who I refer to as Elmira's elite—worked together to welcome prison construction as a source of economic development on a trajectory laid out for them by the federal and state government. The story of this contested terrain of development lays bare the uneasy politics of development.

Elmira was only one of the thousands of places that were seeking out new modes of "job creation" and taxation. David Harvey has argued that a massive transformation in urban governance emerged in the late 1970s, a period that marked a shift in the organization and function of cities. The former managerial mode of urban governance was replaced by a necessarily more entrepreneurial function in an increasingly competitive, globalized world. Cities, particularly cities hit hard by crises of deindustrialization, had to search for new forms of capital influx.[5] Prisons emerged as a solution first to the problem of capital loss for Elmira, while dovetailing with a "solution" acceptable to the local elite and reasonably favorable to the white working-class men who ostensibly would seek jobs there. But while the idea, the plan, and the proposal to expand prisons came from Albany and New York City, they found fertile ground among the elite and their planners in Elmira. Two decades after LBJ's War on Poverty and less than a decade after the Attica Rebellion, the massive expansion of prisons in New York State was built with the bricks of crime talk and job creation while at the same time both the state and New York City were signaling larger shifts in giveaways to corporations and real estate interests.

Throughout the chapter, I focus on the crucial role of the state in determining the paths and modes of economic development in the state of New York and how these processes have unfolded in Elmira. I show the ways that relationships between state and private business became deeply entangled—indeed, inseparable—in an effort to solve the crisis of unemployment and economic loss in Elmira. Prison construction does not create profits for owners as manufacturing did in the past; rather, the prison "boom" infused state capital into Elmira primarily through wages. To a lesser extent, monies from the state also flowed through Department of Corrections contracts with hospitals, food companies, and, at irregular intervals, construction firms. While white working-class Elmirans can hardly be considered elite in a grander sense, it is important to think through how white working-class men, particularly those in law enforcement, can function as both the allies and conduits of elite interests. Largely through "transfer payments" made from the state to the county through the construction and maintenance of prisons that expand the limited wealth— and therefore status and privilege—of some white workers as a "niche" population, the growth coalition secures a secondary gain in the alliance of this group with its own bloc.[6]

William Cronon writes that it is difficult to "draw a boundary between the abstraction called city and the abstraction called country" and calls for writing the two together in a "unified narrative."[7] Elmira exists not just in the outlines of the city on a map but, as critical geographers have taught us, within a web of urban social relationships that are produced, reproduced, and sometimes disguised across the geographic space of New York State through its prison system. With the Attica Rebellion barely in the rear-view mirror and Reaganism on the rise, Elmira—and the two state prisons—were not places "away" from New York State politics but rather at the heart of the coercive power of the state. Prisons were built in order to be filled with the young men who were purported to be the *cause* of the disorder, rather than those who bore the brunt of the cuts to social programs in the newly austere New York. As the crime talk grew louder in Nixon's White House, echoes of the same punitive responses to social upheaval could be heard in Albany and in New York City. From the state Senate Committee on Crime and Correction to the city halls of cities big and small, politicians urged the public to tighten the reins on criminality and talked about overcrowded jails. The decision to criminalize unrest among Black and Brown New Yorkers and the decision to expand the city and state use of prisons fed off each other and grew with the aid of the growing pots of money available at every scale of government to expand prisons and jails.

Historians describe how the seeds of mass incarceration were planted in the period of "postwar racial liberalism" but grew exponentially after the Black freedom movement.[8] Naomi Murakawa writes that the "race problem" of the civil rights movement from the 1940s onward was answered with pledges of carceral state development.[9] There is no natural relationship between crime statistics and penal growth; rather, prisons were what was on offer in the cacophony of transformations in capital accumulation and working-class life in the early 1980s in New York.

The Rockefeller drug laws are often seen as the singular source of prison growth in the 1970s, and indeed the laws were a significant propellant of heightened mass criminalization of Black and Brown New Yorkers.[10] In 1973 Governor Nelson Rockefeller instituted laws calling for new regime of "zero tolerance" for drug crimes, including mandatory sentences for small amounts of drug sale, manufacture, or possession.

These new laws were enacted in a racialized way: while drugs were found to be used equally across racial groups, Black and Latino/a/x people were far more likely to be criminalized for doing so.[11] As Ruth Wilson Gilmore has noted, mass incarceration relies on mass criminalization, an "enormous and daunting process" that "occurs through the enactment of little things."[12] Once the Rockefeller laws were on the books, the day-to-day policing of Black, Brown, and poor New Yorkers occurred in the streets, in the subways, in the schools, and on the roads. But the desire for prison expansion, and, more significantly, the funding for prison expansion, was already in the works.

The Bond Act

In the spring of 1981, an act titled "Security through the Development of Correctional Facilities Bond Act of 1981" (hereafter, the Bond Act) was introduced in the New York State Senate. The Bond Act proposed to sell bonds for the construction of three new prisons to house fifteen hundred additional inmates at the Upstate prisons of Wallkill, Woodburne, and Coxsackie, as well as to raise money for local jails, state troopers, and the expansion of facilities for juveniles. When the Bond Act was first introduced, there were thirty-two prisons holding 23,400 prisoners in New York State, said by the Department of Corrections (DOCS) to be at 104 percent of capacity.[13] In the *New York Times*, the DOCS commissioner described himself as "frantic" in trying to figure out where to put the prisoners, insisting to the press that he might have to put inmates in tents in jail yards.[14] At the same time that the Bond Act was being introduced to the legislature, the guards' union was suing the state over what it considered workplace safety issues in overcrowded prisons. Prisoners' rights advocates, notably the Correctional Association, led the public opposition to the Bond Act and sued the city to push the government to adopt alternatives to incarceration, such as increased funding for drug treatment. But state officials appeared confident that the measure would pass. Indeed, Department of Correctional Services Commissioner Coughlin spoke confidently about the bond issue as a bellwether for public sentiment about crime: "I believe this bond issue will settle this discussion [of the public's ideas about the criminal justice system]. If the people want tougher sentencing, better prosecution, and jail to go along with that, they're going to vote this bond issue in. If this bond issue goes down, then that's a clear indication from the people that they want to start looking at social programs to reduce crime."[15]

Governor Carey and New York City Mayor Koch both stumped for the Bond Act's passage across the state. Koch described the Bond Act as a "put up or shut up" matter: if citizens didn't vote to put the money up for the prisons, then they had better mute their concerns about crime.[16] The state senators and State Assembly largely agreed and the Bond Act was approved by the state senate in July of 1981. Subsequently, however, it was narrowly voted down by the electorate a few months later, in November. The act's defeat by ballot was indicative of a divided electorate: during an uptick in crime, and the ensuing panic stoked by white political leaders from Rockefeller to Carey to Lindsay to Koch, voters in New York City cast their ballots two to one in favor of the measure. But in Upstate New York, the measure was defeated three to two.

Koch made a veiled suggestion that Upstate voters' racism motivated their rejection of the Bond Act: "The measure was defeated by upstate voters who feared the construction of new prisons populated largely by people from New York City."[17] This comment was of course deeply racialized: "big city" crime was associated with the images of Black and Brown voters. My ethnographic work in Elmira suggests that Koch was in some ways correct; many Elmirans viewed their city as immune to such crime and hoped to keep out the "riff raff," even if that meant keeping them behind steel bars and gates.

In fact, both reads of the situation are true: racialized fears of crime and criminality led to the initiative's approval by New York City residents and also to the initiative's rejection in Elmira. In New York City, Koch's law-and-order campaign and apocalyptic crime talk undoubtedly swayed the vote. Upstate, the prison bond vote was the only vote in the history of Chemung County *specifically* dealing with prisons and prison expansion. I consider it an important marker in the record of public opinion and a precursor for the substantive division over prisons as criminal justice policy in the following years. In Chemung County, already the home to the Elmira Correctional Facility, the measure was defeated 52 percent to 48 percent, or 7,301 voting no and 6,633 voting yes.[18] Considering the public's conflicted views of both prisons after the completed construction of Southport Correctional Facility (which I discuss in depth in chapter 4), it is conceivable that an underlying racism, mistrust, and distorted perception of urban-ness was part of the overall rejection of the measure by Upstate voters. My interviews with Elmirans suggest that other forces may have contributed to the voters' rejection of the measure: there was a tiny, religiously based progressive bloc that rejected the growth of prisons as criminal justice policy; a strain of anti-government and conservative populism that rejected increases in government spending; and a hope among many that different jobs, other than prison work, might be created. Robert Geiger, who worked in an alternatives to incarceration program in Elmira, urged others to vote against the Bond Act because he objected to "both the price and the purpose of the new prisons." "And there are alternatives," he told the Elmira *Star-Gazette*.[19] If in 1981 more than 50 percent of residents in a largely conservative county voted against the statewide prison bond, can we assume that there would be significant rejection, as well, of expanding the local prison in their backyards? Following Cronon, and aiming for a unified narrative, we can surmise that the public's defeat of the bond measure and the local politicians' eagerness for the prison together suggest that the city was quite divided about the soon-to-be-constructed prison.

Despite limited public support for the expansion of prisons in New York State, DOCS announced four weeks later that they would still build the proposed prisons. Because there would be no public funding through the selling of state bonds, the state turned to the UDC to fund the construction.[20] Given that it is not a branch of state government like DOCS, the UDC can procure and disburse funding without abiding by state regulations. In 1983 the state legislature authorized the UDC to sell $380 million in bonds to build two state prisons and expand five others. In this way, the prison expansion was advanced through the UDC despite the public's vote against the project. Although this antidemocratic move was fought in court by a wide-ranging group of organizations, including the Nassau Coalition for Safety and Justices, the National Conference of Black Lawyers, and the Fortune Society, the case was dismissed.[21]

Albany and the Urban Development Corporation

The UDC is a public authority established in 1968, charged with the infra-structural economic development of New York State, including public housing and other large-scale development projects like the Jacob Javits Convention Center, the State Office Building in Harlem, and the Battery Park City apartment complex. But during the fiscal crisis of 1975, the UDC went into default; the federal monies that provided the capital for New York's public works dried up. Recovered from that crisis, the UDC made a mark in the late 1970s as a vehicle for what Neil Smith calls a "revan-chist reclamation of space" for the uses of middle-class and bourgeois interests, such as the building of a Hyatt hotel and the transformation of Times Square and Bryant Park in New York City. This is unsurprising, as it was in fact created by the state to enable growth emboldened by a new regime of more beholden real estate developers.[22] As the *New York Times* quipped, "Anyone who wants to see how far the enthusiastic social activism of the 1960's has given way to the sober economic realities of the 1970's need only look at the current activities of the New York State Urban Development Corporation."[23]

The appointment of Vincent Tese, a former state banking director, as chairman and CEO of the UDC in March 1985 was a part of both the aus-terity politics of post—fiscal crisis New York City and the national trend toward embracing neoliberal policies.[24] At the beginning of his term, Tese called for public recognition of the crisis in the political economy of New York State. He outlined a new agenda for the governance of the state's economy, laying the future squarely in the hands of private busi-nesses by following Reagan's plan for tax abatements and relaxed labor regulations. Announcing this new direction, Tese said, "It is axiomatic that the private sector is the engine which drives New York's economy."[25]

In a departure from the 1960s pattern of couching business projects as public works, Tese's major focus was to enhance the "business cli-mate" of New York State. The targeted beneficiaries of his overall eco-nomic strategy were the poorest places in the state, notably Elmira and Utica-Rome upstate, East Harlem in New York City, and Yonkers. Tese's 1985 Strategic Plan for Economic Development in New York State cited the fact that Elmira had lost 50 percent of its manufacturing jobs since

1970; his fantastic plan was to replace those manufacturing losses with jobs in computers and biotechnology, which would be lured to the state via business incentives. Following the Reagan administration's national push for "enterprise zones," Tese created zones around neighborhoods deemed in need of help.[26] At the same time, his tenure marked a shift in the use of the UDC to build new prisons across New York State. Despite the conspicuous absence of prisons in how the UDC and its plan for New York's economic development were presented to the public, thirty-eight new prisons were built between 1971 and 2000, all with investment dollars from UDC proposals for infrastructural growth.

Prison Siting in New York State

Upon Governor Cuomo's announcement in June of 1983 of the planned construction of five new prisons after the legislative approval of the bonds, municipalities across the state began competing for selection as a prison site. The initial proposal announced by Commissioner Coughlin and Governor Cuomo planned for expanding the Upstate prisons at Attica and Great Meadow and for constructing new prisons along the Canadian border, now home to the Clinton Correctional Facility in Dannemara, the state's largest prison. DOCS proposed an additional prison to be built on North Brother Island in the South Bronx just off of Rikers Island. While the Bond Act was electorally more popular in New York City than other parts of the state, it was a thornier political project to build a state prison in the city itself. Like their Upstate counterparts, city politicians were eyeing the construction of a state prison as a jobs plan. Mayor Koch supported the measure, saying, "We [New York City] intend to do our share," citing "the obligation of the city of New York and all other upstate counties to cooperate with the state in the building of state prisons."[27] The commissioner of correctional services said of the chosen spot in the South Bronx, atop a working New York City Transit Authority rail yard, "If there's any place to build a prison in New York City, this is it."[28]

But unlike in Elmira and other locations upstate, New York City politicians were also responding to an organized anti-prison element of the electorate, namely Black and Latino/a/x districts that had the highest numbers of men and women incarcerated in Upstate prisons. State

Assemblyman José Serrano, who represented the Bronx district where the prison was planned to be built, commented, "My initial thought is that the first major statement by the Cuomo Administration about the Bronx is not rebuilding housing stock but building a maximum security-prison."[29] Shortly after Serrano's statement, the site was determined to be too costly. A less-than-warm welcome by local politicians undoubtedly put the project at risk. Mayor Koch lamented the loss of the prison for the Bronx because "it was a hardship for relatives of prisoners from the city to travel hundreds of miles to prisons upstate for visits." It is indeed the case that siting prisons in distant Upstate towns makes it hard for New Yorkers to visit their incarcerated kin. However, Koch's professed empathy for the families of incarcerated men and women is questionable, given his simultaneous desire to compete for economic resources and jobs in a time of economic crisis.

In the end, in addition to concerns over the cost of land in New York City, which is inevitably more expensive than upstate, the Department of Correctional Services chose to build prisons in places that welcomed prison jobs without significant negative public comment. They found that home in Elmira, Chemung County, New York.

A Small City in the Global Economy

Unlike the South Bronx, the city of Elmira and some of the surrounding villages put out the red carpet for the state's economic development elites and the Department of Correctional Services. With the highest unemployment rate on record in New York State and the loss of thousands of manufacturing jobs in the first half of the 1980s, Elmira was in a state of crisis. The dire state of the economy made Elmira a ripe candidate for the state's budding mechanism of economic development: prisons.

When the governor announced that the state was looking for a site to build a new prison, the County Planning Board and the local economic development agency, Southern Tier Economic Growth (STEG), sprang into action in Elmira. The STEG director told a reporter, "We will do whatever we have to do" to get the prison built in Elmira.[30] Eager for growth, Elmira's growth coalition coalesced to encourage the construction of a prison in the county and dispel any notion of local opposition. In July 1985 the Chemung County Legislature passed a resolution titled

"Favoring the Construction of a 500-Bed Prison Adjacent to the Elmira Correctional Facility."[31]

The resolution framed the prison expansion as a jobs issue, beginning with, "WHEREAS, the New York State Department of Corrections has indicated a need for two additional maximum security prisons in upstate New York, to house 500 inmates each" and continuing, "WHEREAS, it is estimated that 430 new jobs would be created by building an additional prison facility, thereby alleviating the severe economic decline this area has experienced recently."[32] The wording of the measure framed the debate in terms that would be difficult to challenge in a time of financial crisis. There were no public comments made regarding the resolution, and it passed unanimously.

A few months later, in September, the Elmira City Council voted unanimously to urge Cuomo and DOCS Commissioner Coughlin to build the prison in Elmira.[33] The local boosters put it bluntly to Cuomo and the DOCS administration: to build a prison in Elmira was to support Upstate. The mayor-elect penned a letter to DOCS and Cuomo that read, "For too long Elmira has been continually devastated by the poor economic conditions of the region. There is no better time than now to show your support for Elmira and your commitment to the Southern Tier."[34] Their campaign worked: in September of 1985, the Elmira area was formally declared a preferred site for the construction of a new prison by the Department of Correctional Services.

A New Coalition for Growth

After the Elmira area was selected as a preferred site, a new growth coalition in the city of Elmira emerged, united by a common commitment to prison expansion as a means of economic development. In smaller cities like Elmira, the local elite is not made up of global bankers or uberwealthy politicians, but rather of regional politicians, business owners, and their allies who use their resources to shape the flow of capital into the area. For example, STEG, the local economic development nonprofit mentioned earlier, raised more than one-quarter of its funds from local businesses.[35] In the period of proposal and construction of new prisons, STEG and its allies made a further and more importance alliance with powerful actors pushing for growth in Albany, including but not limited to the governor, Goldman Sachs, and New York City politicians, who each had their own stake in the expansion of prisons.

In the week following the announcement that the Elmira area had been selected, the editors of the Elmira *Star-Gazette* pleaded for unity in the next stage of choosing a specific location for the prison:

> Great!
>
> Call Elmira a prison town, call us anything you want.
>
> But one thing we can add is that a spirit of cooperation has helped us to land a big victory. Thursday's announcement that the state plans to build a second maximum security facility here means a fat new payroll—400 jobs.
>
> Now we need the same community unity that helped persuade Gov. Mario Cuomo and state leaders to build a multi-million dollar prison here. We must work together to build a suitable location.
>
> Some opposition is likely to spring up over the prison site. Let's hope people will be sensible during any debate and look beyond individual or parochial interests for the betterment of the entire region.
>
> After all, being a prison town for years hasn't really been such a hardship. Many residents hardly think of the "Hill" unless they happen to drive by or see it in the news.
>
> As we recover from the loss of smoke-stack industries, the transition to more of a service-oriented economy will be helped along by the prison.
>
> It will result in the development of more housing and businesses. Although prosperity won't come in a burst, it can be nurtured along by community unity. The state has handed us the ball and it's time to run with it.[36]

When Governor Cuomo formally announced the selection of Southport as the site, an editorial in the *Star-Gazette* trumpeted it as a "double dose of good news."[37] The paper gave a "formal tip of the Tier hat . . . to Governor Cuomo for fulfilling a commitment to help troubled areas of the state" and added, "Considering all of the advantages of being a two-prison town the greatest of these is the creation of jobs."[38]

With this editorial and others, the city's only newspaper molded the narrative of what it meant to be a prison town. The piece suggested that the "betterment" of the region was bound up in the expansion of Elmira's role in the New York State prison system. Moreover, it positioned the prison as the *only choice* for the region, the only resolution to the instability of working people's lives in Elmira, and the only path to security for equally nervous local elites. At a time when people were imagining a future without the "smoke-stack industries," the paper was also issuing a warning: What would happen if Elmira didn't have a new prison? What would come next? If we take the 1981 statewide bond vote as an indication of the public's unease about prison expansion, the work of the newspaper here becomes all the more necessary and important: the paper sought to create a "common sense" of the prison's construction in the city, that its placement would be a necessary part of municipal rebirth.[39]

Within Chemung County, various players competed for the siting of the prison, including the village of Horseheads, the town of Southport, and the town of Veteran. The state required that the location have ready access to sewer and water lines, which would be built and maintained by the "host" county. Rumors flew about where and when the new prison would come to Elmira, as local politicians and development officials searched for the perfect site. Among the first proposals for the new prison site, as was noted in the Chemung County Legislature referendum, was a parcel of land next to the ECF, but it was rejected for being "too hilly."[40] The same day, the *Star-Gazette* reported that the governor was looking for a site with a type of soil that doesn't freeze as quickly and therefore allows for a longer construction season, a kind of soil not found within Elmira's boundaries.[41] Despite the competition, there appeared to be consensus among key figures in the growth coalition—STEG, State Assemblyman George Winner, Chemung County legislators, and the editors of the *Star-Gazette*—that land held publicly should be used for the prison so as to not decrease the tax base.

In December 1985 there were four locations under consideration: the abandoned Ann Page Foods (A & P) plant in the village of Horseheads, near the ever-expanding shopping mall; a defunct hockey arena owned by Elmira College in the town of Veteran, just north of Elmira; a private parcel of land also in Veteran; and a privately owned piece of farmland in the town of Southport. The town board of Veteran voted against the prison's construction, citing "environmental concerns" about the swamp lands and the possible lack of water supply. In response, State Assemblyman Winner, the co-chair of the Republican Task Force on the Corrections Crisis, collected 360 signatures in support of the prison, with which he hoped to counterbalance the town board's rejection. But there was additional concern that the area around the prison would lose its property value; despite the assemblyman's effort, it was deemed that there was too much opposition to the site, and it was removed from the list.[42] In the midst of the discussion about various venues for the location of Elmira's second prison, the *Star-Gazette* editors addressed "Albany" directly: "In case you're reading this, Albany, be advised: True, people here have been scrapping over a prison site. True, some will be disappointed by whatever decisions you make, but it's time to bite the bullet. We can take it. Honest."[43] The piece tried to send a clear message to the state capital and anyone opposed to the prison locally that NY State Assembly member Randy Kuhl, Winner, STEG, and local business owners were all in agreement that a new prison would be good for Elmira and good for the region's workers.

In February 1986 the farmland in Southport was chosen as the site of a new prison. Unlike the town of Veteran, the Town of Southport's planning board and many area businesses had gone out of their way to welcome the prison and encourage its construction. DOCS Commissioner Coughlin replied in kind, speaking of his hopes for a "long and profitable relationship" between DOCS and the Town of Southport through the Southport Correctional Facility.[44] Southport's town supervisor, Bob Masia, was central to the courting of DOCS; upon his retirement, he said that he counted the construction of the Southport Correctional Facility among his greatest accomplishments in public service.[45] "Institution Road," the road built as the entrance to the new prison, was formally changed to Bob Masia Drive following his death in 2007. Masia was eulogized for having done a great deal for the area: he owned Masia's Restaurant, was a thirty-year volunteer firefighter, and served on the town's Enterprise Zone Council.[46] But primarily, he took credit for his boosterism for the prison.

Despite the mantra of "jobs, jobs, jobs," local politicians and other boosters had to work to create an image of future wealth and prosper-

FIG. 2. A local business congratulates the town of Southport, adjacent to Elmira, on the planned siting of a new prison in New York State. George Lian, *Elmira Star-Gazette*, February 22, 1986, A1. Star-Gazette—USA TODAY NETWORK.

ity linked to the new prison. A picture in the *Star-Gazette* shows that some area businesses supported the prison construction; the day after Albany's announcement, a sign reading "Congratulations Southport, we got the prison!" was outside of a Southport restaurant.[47] But perhaps the most powerful example of this kind of image is a photo published in the *Star-Gazette* the day following the groundbreaking for the site: it depicts the granddaughter of a Southport councilman, a smiling white toddler in a white bonnet, sitting next to a shovel labeled "Chemung Correctional Facility."

The choice to place a child in this picture serves both to elide the human cost of incarceration and prison work and to disguise the ugliness of the project. At the same time the child represents many of the workers' worst fears: their inability to provide for their own children. Abstracted from the social death of the prison and prison work, the prison is represented as public good.

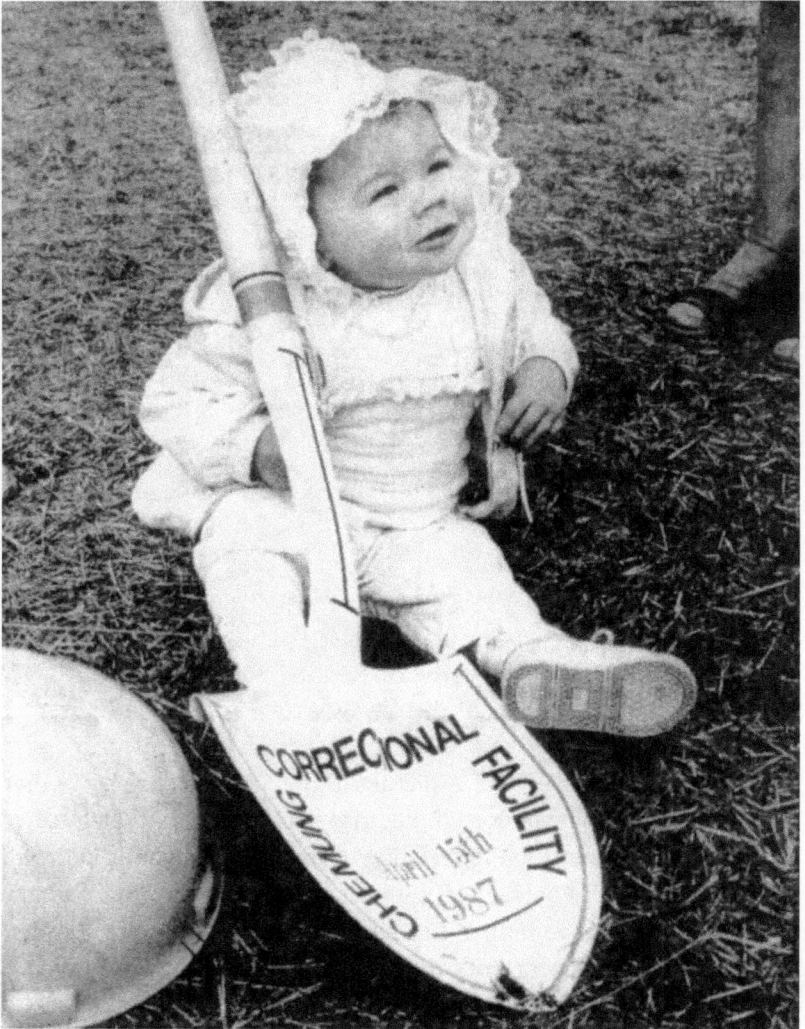

FIG. 3. The granddaughter of a city councilmember, is posed with a shovel at the groundbreaking ceremony of the new prison, later to be renamed the Southport Correctional Facility. George Lian, *Elmira Star-Gazette*, April 16, 1987, B1. Star-Gazette—USA TODAY NETWORK.

Shortening the Road Home for Elmira's Workers

While not a centerpiece in the public propaganda regarding prison construction, the correction officers' union, AFSCME Council 82, supported the prison expansion in Elmira and across the state. (The independent union that represents the correction officers today, NYSCOPBA, remains a powerful lobbying force in opposition to prison closures.) At the individual level, correction officers hailing from Elmira but working in prisons elsewhere in the state regarded the construction of the second prison as a development that would improve their lives, as it would allow them to commute less and spend more time with their families. At the time of the Southport selection, the ECF was reported to have one of the largest transfer lists in the state, meaning that there were men and women working as guards in prisons across the state and waiting to earn enough seniority to bid for a job at their "hometown jail." According to one guard working at Groveland Correctional Facility, a medium security prison about eighty miles from Elmira, Groveland was referred to as "Elmira II" because there were so many guards commuting there from Elmira and neighboring towns.[48] Workers carpooled the three-hour daily commute until they gained enough seniority to land a job at the ECF. This indicates that large numbers of people in Elmira were already working for DOCS before the Southport Correctional Facility was built, and that the construction of Southport was clearly in the interest of these workers.

Prisons and Enterprise Zones

The growth in corrections jobs may have ameliorated the conditions of some workers, but there were still many men and women left out of the mainstream economy in Elmira. After years of disinvestment by the federal government and the loss of thousands of manufacturing jobs, new neoliberal policies took form in the building of more public prisons and the awarding of tax abatements and incentives to private companies. These were also offered as solutions to very different parts of New York State, which varied in their demographics, geography, and the specificity of their postindustrial experience. While they seem to be opposite sides of the coin—one the expansion of "public work" in prisons, and the other giveaways to corporations—these urban/rural development plans dovetailed in Elmira in the notion of rejecting "municipal welfare." That is, local development officials followed the state line: pursue privatization while growing punitive state projects. In one embodiment of this phenomenon, head of the UDC Tese was highly involved in all of these projects, from prison siting to more traditional UDC activities like finding tenant businesses for the massive, abandoned A & P plant.

In a public hearing in Chemung County in February 1985 on the formation of enterprise zones in New York State, local public officials, businesspeople, and advocates for the unemployed described a desperate situation in the city of Elmira and the surrounding areas: the highest unemployment rate in the state, the loss of thousands of manufacturing jobs, and the shrinking tax base. Facing the loss of the federal grant monies to cities—part of the national pattern—local politicians and their growth coalition partners were equally desperate for assistance from the state.[49] Following the entrepreneurial rhetoric of the era, the mayor of Elmira stated that the city was not looking for "municipal welfare" but rather for an opportunity to thrive, insisting that "we have done everything we can to help ourselves."[50] The head of STEG pleaded, "Instead of becoming liabilities and cost and burdens to the state, we feel that this area can be taxpayers, they can be part of a healthy strong economy that makes a contribution to the state and doesn't have to be a burden to the state."[51] These proposals for enterprise zones coincided with Reagan's anti-welfare rampage, the rhetoric of which is quite visible within the discussion of the enterprise zone. State giveaways to private companies in the form of tax abatements and wage subsidies are not construed as "welfare," a word stained with racialized connotations of lazy people who get stuff for free. (In chapter 3, I explore this notion and fear of dependency in depth.)

What emerged from the public hearing about the possibilities of creating an enterprise zone in Chemung County is a picture of the political economy of Elmira on February 26, 1986. Elmira had an unemployment rate of 16 percent. One-third of the people in the proposed zone carved out of the city's lost manufacturing sector lived below the poverty line. The numbers of Elmirans on public assistance had increased by 25 percent in four years (New York State and Smith 1986). The hours of testimony from growth coalition boosters from across the Southern Tier, including the Kennedy Valve fire hydrant plant operations manager and representatives from Conrail and the Southern Tier Regional Planning Board, were filled with pleadings for an influx of capital and hope for the future of their cities and towns.

Two final presentations from members of the Greater Elmira Unemployment Council and the Pine City chapter of the National Unemployment Council re-centered the discussion on jobs. The Elmira council noted that none of the planning for the enterprise zones had involved unemployed workers and cautioned that legislators introduced something new every year and nothing seemed to work. The Pine City group reminded Assemblyman Winner that giving public subsidies to corporations in an attempt to anchor private companies was not a new tactic in Elmira. In fact, through the federal UDAG (Urban Development Action Grant) program, American LaFrance had been given two million dollars to stay in Elmira and keep its jobs there, but they still, shortly thereafter, moved their production to South Carolina.[52] The "American LaFrance fiasco," as all parties referred to it during the hearing served as an example of how local people were swindled. During the same period, a twenty-year tax abatement was given to Toshiba Westinghouse to relocate to Elmira. This company subsequently closed the factory in the late 1990s, before its twenty years were up. The only incentive given to a company in the 1980s that might be considered successful was a $1.8 million given to Diamond-Bathhurst Corporation to keep open the doors of Thatcher Glass (now Anchor Glass Container Corporation), which is still a viable manufacturer in Elmira. The UDAG was eliminated by President Reagan, and enterprise zones subsequently became a popular state response to the crisis. The voices of advocates for the unemployed were raised in a comparably empty chamber. They were more or less overshadowed by the previous crowd's eagerness to get to the task at hand: capitalist urban development.

In their application to create an enterprise zone, the city of Elmira proposed to use economic development funds from the state to expand daycare, build roads and bridges, and give incentives to lure new businesses back to the area.[53] How did the focus on basic infrastructure in Elmira's application to create an enterprise zone fit into the architecture of the UDC's enterprise zones as spearheaded by Tese? The latter model of development insisted on the need to "make them compete" and "make the counties throw in some goodies that we need."[54] As George Winner, a prominent local conservative asked at the hearing, "How will the poorest counties compete?"[55] Elmira's first round request to create an empowerment zone was denied. The state later expanded the program and Elmira was included in the project. The construction of the Southport Correctional Facility fulfilled the state's duty to "help out" the Elmira area and the many other prison towns, new and old, dotting the Upstate rust belt.

Are Three Prisons Too Many?

The only "growth industry" of any economic or political consequence that took root in Elmira in the 1980s was that of state prisons. Cuomo's first $1 billion Department of Corrections budget in 1987 did not go unnoticed by State Assemblyman Winner or State Senator Randy Kuhl. Just as plans were being finalized for the Southport Correctional Facility site, the *Star-Gazette*'s headline informed its readers of the possibility of a new prison: "Tug of War Begins for Prison Site."[56] Another competition began as more state investment dollars were announced to expand the prison system. Winner optimistically responded, "We're talking about a growth industry here" and suggested that the prison already promised to the Elmira area could expand from 400 beds to 750 beds.[57]

But the possibility of a third prison revealed a fissure in the local growth coalition. The local paper, which had been a steady supporter of prisons as an engine for local development, changed its tone: "Jobs are important, but at some point, the negatives of a prison outweigh the job benefits."[58] Three prisons, the editorial board of the *Star-Gazette* wrote, were too many.[59] The editorial board—and undoubtedly other businesspeople who made up the growth coalition—preferred to project an image of "Mark Twain County." They envisioned marketing Elmira as a tourist destination built around the fact that Elmira is where Twain wrote his great books, and where he lived and died with his wife, the daughter of Elmira's wealthiest businessman. The notion that the prison industry precludes other kinds of development, particularly tourism, has remained a constant tension in the political economy of Elmira (and other prison towns) over the past three decades. However, the newspaper changed its tune a few months later: the new prison would be a "nice nugget for the Tiers."[60] This change had to do with the rumored site of the third prison: the shuttered A & P plant. Until it was leveled in 2006–2007, the plant was a constant reminder of the area's manufacturing decline. The symbolism of using the A & P plant rather than constructing a new prison cannot be underestimated: it was quite literally a vision based on retooling the factories to create something else deemed socially productive. Like many other deindustrializing places, cities and citizens sought to make use of spaces and places that had gone fallow.[61] In the end, while the Southport Correctional Facility was constructed as planned, another area of the state was chosen for the next prison.

Searching for Opposition

Over the course of my fieldwork, I wondered to what extent local residents had been opposed to the construction of the Southport Correctional Facility, and how they conveyed such opposition. I eagerly asked local advocates of prison reform if they had voiced any concerns about or resistance to the construction of new prisons. I found that people had mostly kept their opposition to themselves. The push for prison construction seemed to have come from Albany, including via representatives with strong ties to the area, and businesses and local civic groups seemed relatively resigned to the fact of prison expansion. While the union of correction officers, NYSCOPBA, may have been a silent (but active) supporter of the prison, there were many silent, inactive detractors. I asked Priscilla Moore, who volunteered inside the prison via her church, "What did you think when they opened Southport?" She replied, "It was just, 'Oh yeah, it's a lot of jobs,' but look at the cost of these people in these jobs. What's really happening? What's giving them the jobs? And [what] if there could be something else that we could do to prevent another prison and create more jobs?"

Many I spoke with, both detractors and supporters of prison expansion, spoke frankly about the area's economic problems and the choice to use prisons for economic development. Reverend Ruben Johnson, a Black pastor of a local AME church, said, "Well, people didn't want that [Southport built]. They didn't want Southport here. The citizens were against it and they still are. But they can't do nothing about it." While he had not voiced opposition to prison construction, a white local businessman recalled graffiti on the retaining wall by the Chemung River in downtown Elmira: "Cowards Build Prisons." In his estimation, Upstate's place in the New York State economy was linked to the construction of prisons: "The upstate area can be used for a dumping ground for garbage or violent offenders, or really anything." According to Maria Adamzisk, a white woman whose husband was incarcerated in another part of the state, the town of Southport requested that the prison's name, originally to be "Chemung Correctional Facility," be changed to "Southport Correctional Facility." She chuckled at the thought, incredulous that the village would seek such an honor.

Irene Simons, a white college professor active in many local causes, recalled the history of the Southport facility: "At the opening of Southport, I don't think any people wanted a second large prison here, and then there was some fear about the fact that it was going to be a maxi-maxi. And then there was a kind of little riot over there. Then there was the idea that the lethal injections or death penalty would be exacted and a number of us resisted that by weekly vigils and things." Having been almost run over by a worker on the road to the prison during one of those vigils, she noted, "I don't know how much effect we had." These silences are indicative of a larger culture of fatalism: in the climate of the period, the construction of the Southport prison was considered inevitable.

3 Doing My Zero to Eight

In the spring of 2008, I sat with two white men, Brian Newman and Roy Lewis, who had retired after working as correction officers at the Elmira Correctional Facility together for over thirty years, in a small room of the Southside Community Center. The men were in their late fifties, both wearing jeans and button-down shirts. I had interviewed Brian previously, and he asked if I would be interested in talking to his old partner as well. The men were friendly and comfortable.

For Brian, a career correction officer who was hired in 1980, the racial and geographic divisions of New York State prisons were a part of his work from the day he entered the prison. He said, "I dealt with mostly New York City inmates in my career [that spanned from 1980 to 2008]. They were all from Rikers Island and they hated Elmira. They hated— when they were sentenced to Elmira and the judge says, you're going to Elmira, it was a word that just triggered their—they hated it here. They were scared to death." Brian narrates the experience of prisoners hating a particular place—Elmira, his home—rather than hating their incarceration. He asserts that the geography is part of the punishment and that more than fearing incarceration the inmates feared being sent away to a place unlike their homes and guarded by a group of men who saw themselves as both culturally distinct and superior. He continued:

> They were scared to death to come to Elmira. Why? I don't know. It had a reputation that way . . . As being a tougher—they didn't take any bologna here. They just didn't take a lot of bologna here. They didn't—the bigger cities were the—and I've worked in places like this, say, for example the—we have a problem. Well, this guy's from the same area that I live in, in New York City. He lives in the projects,

I live over here, he knows me, he knows my family. Well, I'm gonna have a different rapport with him than I'm going to have with a person that I have no contact with and never will have contact with other than being in the prison.

In this construct, successful guarding—"not taking any bologna"—requires a similar background among guards, one distinct from that of the Black and Brown prisoners from the city. While Brian never noted this specifically, the description suggests that he meant men like him, white men, or perhaps more specifically, white men from small towns and rural areas of Upstate New York.

The "rapport" that Brian perceives correction officers from New York City having with prisoners violates the common sense, both among security staff and state level bureaucracies, of corrections: don't get too friendly, be aware of how inmates could possibly be deceiving you at all times, and sweep every corner for potential dangers.[1] It is possible that Brian makes this assumption based on the downstate prisoners' and guards' shared urban background. More likely, considering that 75 percent of correction officers at Sing Sing Correctional Facility just north of New York City, the archetypal downstate prison, are Black or Latino/a/x, Brian presumes that one's racial identity, one's Blackness or Latinidad, brings one closer to the projects, to the storied "inner-city" streets, and to the core hegemonic American ideas of criminality.[2]

The ECF is a part of the physical infrastructure of the state—steel bars, cement, walls, cages, and an arsenal—but prisons are maintained by both the labor of the men incarcerated there and the labor of the men and women who do the physical work of containment. This work, both the work of basic social reproduction and the physical work of control, is done by people who are connected to the cultures, histories, and political economies in which they were raised, what Elmirans often call one's "hometown." While across the country the racial topography is not uniform, the use of racial divides to "order" the relationships between prisoner and guard have a long history both in the United States and across the globe.[3] The security personnel at the ECF and the Southport Correctional Facility are 96 percent white and the incarcerated population is roughly 75 percent Black and Latino/a/x. Roediger and Esch use the frame of "race management" to describe bosses' use of cultural, linguistic, and geographic differences—racial by systemic design—to maintain control over a workplace.[4] I extend that frame to the prison as a place of work for correction officers and as a place where prisoners are removed from the possibility of wage labor. Through the incarceration of tens of thousands of largely Black and Latino/a/x people in the prime of their working lives while recruiting white men to guard them, the state further enshrines the racialized labor hierarchies of the past in and through the New York State prison system. Prisons are a workplace that through its brutal differentiations reproduces Blackness and whiteness, thus maintaining Fordism's labor hierarchies in a retooled racialization as jailer and jailed.

Whiteness is fundamentally about a set of group advantages. Roediger builds on Du Bois's argument that while white workers have "received a low wage [they were] compensates in part by a . . . public and psychological wage."[5] Roediger writes, "As important as the specifics are here, still more important is the idea that the pleasures of whiteness could function as a 'wage' for white workers. That is, status and privileges conferred by race could be used to make up for alienating and exploitative class relationships, North and South. White workers could, and did, define and accept their class positions by fashioning identities as 'not slaves' and as 'not Blacks.'"[6] For thousands of white Upstaters, the expansion of the carceral state fortified and expanded an adage on this list: "Not a prisoner."

And yet, the whiteness of Upstate prison guards is useful for the state but has limited advantages for the white guards themselves. While gaining a preferential relationship to the state and a "middle class" lifestyle through state prison employment, prison guards make complicated trades in other forms of stigma. I argue that both the violent work of physically controlling prisoners deemed out of line and the mundane work of social reproduction and control (delivering meals to those in solitary, walking concrete floors, shooing men into cages, enforcing asinine rules, watching men play chess and basketball) are essential to upholding the current configuration of racial capitalism that serves sometimes meager advantages to some white workers while robbing millions of people— Black, Brown, and poor white—of their freedom. Though much scholarship has focused on the racial formation of Blackness through the criminal justice system, the relational formation of whiteness through the carceral state remains to be systematically explored.[7] My ethnography shows fractured relationships to belonging, race, labor, and identity among white prison guards as they are recruited to do the work of "race management" in the creation and recreation of racial capitalism.

At Elmira and Southport Correctional Facilities, the correction officers are 97 percent white men, and according to my ethnographic data, largely from Elmira and the rural surrounding areas. There are fourteen hundred men are incarcerated at the ECF, and, until 2022 when it closed, eight hundred men at Southport Correctional Facility. NYS prisoners are 75 percent Black and Latino/a/x, hailing from all over the state, but particularly from New York City, Rochester, and Syracuse.[8] The Elmira situation is a bit of an outlier: among security personnel (correction officers, or, as I prefer to use the colloquial term, prison guards, and their direct supervisors) in prisons and jails across the United States, Black people are overrepresented as prison workers *and* as prisoners, at roughly 13 percent of the U.S. population and 25.5 percent of people employed as security personnel in prisons and jails.[9] For reasons that range from the particular history of New York State and the historical use of Upstate as a part of the regime of punishment, the roles of white guards and Black and Brown prisoners in Elmira and Southport reflect a pattern of experience in the New York State prison system as a whole: 78.6 percent of New York State correction officers are white men. That number climbs slightly to 83.7 percent white if you include white men and white women together. 10.9 percent of correction officers in New York State are Black.[10] This racial pattern shifts based on geography, as prisons closer to New York City, such as the infamous Sing Sing, are characterized by majority Black and Latino/a/x guards.[11]

A Racialized Brotherhood

In a study of correction officers conducted in the late 1970s by a sociologist at Auburn Prison, seventy miles from Elmira, one officer mentioned that the training at the Correctional Services Training Academy explicitly covered the negative public view of correction officers—and how to overcome it with brotherhood.[12] The newly minted guards were told that "people don't think much of you," but, the officer explained, the trainers "try to show you how corrections officers stick together."[13] Lombardo details how prison guards and police often describe the bonds of trust necessary to physically harm prisoners with impunity—to have one another's backs—as a brotherhood. The geography of prison sitings and employment of white working-class Upstaters fortifies the racial element of this brotherhood among prison guards.

This racialized brotherhood was a significant part of how my interlocutors experienced the work of being a guard at the ECF. Brian recalled, "I worked with a tighter knit group of officers that were all—went to school together. Grew up together. Knew each other. Knew each other's family, which is a hometown prison like Elmira." Brian elaborated: a hometown prison was "run by people from Elmira. Most of the guys— I'd say 90 percent were from Elmira. Where, when I worked downstate, they were from all over. But most of them were from the New York City area, which lived with the element that they were watching. Where, in my case, we weren't like that." While there has long been an association of police work with brotherhood, the geographic density of security work in the prison adds a place-based dimension to the notion.[14] According to my interlocutors, working in a hometown prison created camaraderie and safety for them because the guards were more likely to know one another through family networks and local social circles, facilitating closer bonds at work. As Brian's description of the culturally, regionally distinct aspect of working in the ECF makes clear, the guards' *difference* from incarcerated men was the underlying condition for their brotherhood.

Jeff Morton, a white prison guard who has worked in prisons across New York State for more than twenty years, describes the ECF as a place where other guards could be trusted:

> Downstate was different than up here. Up here everybody in Elmira, 99.9 percent you can trust 'em. They didn't run from a fight. If you were in a bad situation, they were there with you. They didn't run. When I was at Greenhaven, the rule was that the guys coming in, you trusted the guys from Elmira, you trusted the guys from Clinton, Dannemora up north—you trusted the guys from Attica. Those three

prisons. If you were upstate and when you ask someone where they were from, and they said Elmira, they'd back you up.

Correction Officer Michael Morgan, also white, describes what it was like to start at the ECF for training and then move on to a downstate prison for his first job assignment: "Now when I became a guard, okay, the need for officers was downstate New York. And what you did was they put you where they want you. First, they put you at your home facility for six weeks of an on-the-job training and then they shipped you to where they wanted you." His "home facility," Elmira, he experienced as "cliquish," that is, uncomfortable "if you are not known. If your friend doesn't work there. If you don't have a relation who works there." And it wasn't until he was introduced around by a relative that "I was then okay, I wasn't somebody that was [pause] . . . I was somebody that could be trusted. That stuff could be done in front of me and it wasn't questioned." Michael described in detail how he beat prisoners and colluded with his fellow officers to cover up the evidence, with the implicit approval of the prison administration. For Michael, the brotherhood of the hometown prison provided guards with impunity for participation in the extralegal, but nonetheless everyday brutality of prison.

COs bring their racial ideas into their work as guards; in doing so, whiteness is not a static fact but remixes with the "race management" of the U.S. prison system. For example, Michael stated quite clearly that his experiences as a correction officer heightened his racialization of prisoners and of people more generally:

> When I went to Watkins Glen School District, there was a class of about six hundred people. Out of that six hundred people, there were like eight or nine Black people. I was never exposed to Black people. When I walked into a mess hall at Elmira Correctional Facility and there were four or five hundred Black people all yelling and screaming and eating lunch, it was an intimidating factor. Until you got used to it and knew how to handle it. I don't really view myself as a ra . . . I don't walk down the road and see a Black man there and have the urge to shoot him, okay? I don't. That has never been part of my . . . okay. But you are predisposed to thinking, are they good or are they bad?

Considering that the population of New York State's prisons is roughly 50 to 60 percent Black, it is remarkable that Morgan remembers the mess hall as a Black place and likely indicative of a racialized perception of Black inmates as more threatening than white inmates.

For the handful of Black guards employed at Elmira and Southport, the brotherhood's protections were fraught. William Jennings, who was one of the first Black guards at Elmira in the 1960s and the only Black guard for a nine-year period through the Attica Rebellion, said that when he began the job at Auburn Correctional Facility his fellow correction officers refused to explain to him how to do the job and he was forced to rely on the inmates to explain the jail protocols to him. For example, he had to ask an inmate to explain the facility's process for moving inmates to mess hall. "Let me tell you what they did to me at Auburn. At Auburn it was a family affair, with their brothers and cousins, and what had happened to me—I had to ask the inmates. Because your coworkers won't tell you? Nothin.' Nothin.'" William assumed that conditions would improve when he gained enough seniority to return to work in Elmira, where he was born and raised, but found that he was not included in the brotherhood of white prison guards there, either.

> When I went back to Elmira, I thought, "This was really a redneck" . . . I should be back at Auburn, it ain't no different. I ain't talking about no strangers, I went to school with these guys . . . And eventually, after a while when they knew that no matter what, that's still gonna be Mr. Jennings, and it worked out good because I—and I tried to explain, we're not gonna have dinner together, I'm not gonna marry your daughter, you ain't gonna marry my son, and as long as we got that straight thing were all right. But I had—I got some good friends now that worked there.

Maintaining social segregation outside of the prison, William thought, was the price for limited entry into the brotherhood of guards.

"Just a Prison Guard"

Despite the access to the middle-income salary and benefits that work in the state prison system provides, correction officers often balance this "affluence" with what they see as the general drudgery of the work, the threat of danger, and their friends' and neighbors' perceptions of their job. Many described a feeling of being undervalued or misunderstood while simultaneously expressing pride that they provide well for themselves and their families.[15] This tension emerges in everyday conversation. For example, when talking about how many people don't understand the good that the prisons do for Elmira, Phillip Kahan defensively pointed to all of the new trucks and suvs in the employee parking lot at the ECF. This parking lot is easily seen from Davis Street, a main thoroughfare through Elmira to the neighboring village of Elmira Heights. The cars and trucks were, to him, a symbol of workers' success and their important contributions to the regional economy. Phillip was a well-paid blue-collar worker and struggled with how others saw his decision to work at what he repeatedly called a "shitty job" with low prestige. "I've talked to so many people that don't make anywhere near the money that I do, don't have anywhere near the benefits I do, and might bitch about their situation but say, 'I would never do what you do.' It's like, I'd rather be poor. I'd rather be in debt, than become a prison guard." Like many other correction officers, Phillip made $70,000 a year including overtime pay. Considering that the average home value in Elmira was just under $85,000 in the spring of 2018, making homes even in the tonier middle-income neighborhoods of West Elmira and Horseheads accessible to the average prison worker, this is the kind of salary that he described to me as "hard to pass up."[16]

Phillip spoke openly about his job, but he was self-deprecating on the topic of his career:

> For me, it was a thing of last resort for everybody. I mean, I'm not that (hesitates) I mean, I'm proud of what I do, but it's almost like, you know, you couldn't do anything else. In some aspects. I mean I look at it, I drive to and from work in my uniform and I might stop at the store in the morning and get coffee or something but I would never . . . but there's guys that go up to the mall and wear their uniform. It's not that I'm ashamed of what I do, but almost. Because number one, people don't understand what we do. They have no clue.

FIG. 4. A husband and wife from Erin, New York, listen to Department of Corrections officials talk about upcoming exams for Correction Officer, Elmira Correctional Facility Clubhouse. Jeff Richards, *Elmira Star-Gazette*, March 1, 1995, A1. Star-Gazette—USA TODAY NETWORK.

When I asked if he felt like his uniform marked him, he continued, "It just . . . yeah, I'm a loser, look at me. I couldn't make it in the real world, so I had to become a prison guard."

Another guard, George Hanley, also said he did not wear his uniform in public and made fun of other guards he saw wearing theirs outside of the workplace, adding, "C'mon—you're just a prison guard." George said he avoided talking about his job publicly. When strangers asked what kind of work he did, George said he "worked for the state." A third guard, Gordon Gaughan, remembered taking the job as a young man in the '80s because he had a difficult time finding work with his sociology degree and wanted a "nice car." The tone in his voice, a fatalism, suggested that this was a decision that carried some regret. Feeling like a "failure" in relation to those who have "succeeded" in a competitive capitalist and deeply unequal economy is an aspect of working-class identity that has been repeatedly captured by social scientists; however, for some correction officers, a sense of "failure" seems to stem from the nature of security work regardless of the achievement of a middle-class lifestyle.[17] Despite what many guards described as intergenerational legacies of prison work—including having grandfathers, fathers, sons, cousins who all "on the Hill," as the ECF is often called—my interlocutors desperately hoped their sons would not follow in their footsteps: being a correction officer was not viewed as an achievement.

While he considered it a "good job," John complained that other COS took their positions for granted.

> No cause they can't get any other job, especially one that pays like that with a high school . . . hell with a GED. Go to someplace with a GED, yeah after seven years I'd like to be making $60,000 with six weeks paid vacation, 50 percent pension in twenty-five years and kick ass medical benefits that you'd pay about $150 a month for, your kids get a pair of eyeglasses every year, you get one every two years. You, your wife, whatever. Yeah you gotta pay $7 now for a prescription, it might be ten, so what . . . Go to someplace with a high school diploma and tell them that's what you want. I mean, it's not gonna happen. And that's what a lot of guys don't understand. They bitch and moan about the job. And I said, well fine. It sucks so bad here, go take your little high school diploma from Horseheads and tell them what you want.

Two decades after the opening of the Southport Correctional Facility, I found prison workers and local politicians somewhat defensive about the value of the two prisons to Elmira. Without the prisons, a local refrain goes, there would be no jobs at all. And yet, the jobs provided by the prison—the prize promised to Elmira by the state in a time of chaos and crisis—did not and cannot save all the residents of a city in fiscal crisis in 2019 or live up to the fictions of a rebuilt Fordism. The "fragile affluence" of some workers in the Fordist period was traded for prison work. For prison guards across Upstate New York, whiteness is an endless handshake between the "psychological wage" of white supremacy and real wages—the ability to buy a nice car when others can't, to be on the other side of the bars.[18]

"Nothing that You Can Be Proud Of"

Within the notion that prison guards felt misunderstood as "just a prison guard," two themes emerged in my interviews: first, prison guards themselves felt that corrections work in prisons was not "productive work," and second, the guards are often rightfully associated with the brutality of the prison. Michael Morgan explained to me that "not making anything" accounts for a crucial aspect of the experience of a prison guard. Michael said:

> The other thing that goes on with being a prison guard and I think this is one of the biggest problems . . . [He asks me: "What are you going to be when you grow up?" "Me," I ask? "Yeah." "A professor," I say.] Okay, professor. At the end of your day, or your semester, or your year, if you do your job right, you have produced a viable product, something that you could be proud of that you built. Whether it's the character in your students or their learning abilities or that one student who was giving you trouble and you grabbed them by the hand and helped them along. As a prison guard, you produce no product, you have nothing that you can be proud of at the end of the day. It's not there. So, it's not the same as working in a factory and saying yeah, that's my transmission out there in that car. So, there's nothing that you can produce that is something that you can be proud of.

This experience is not exclusive to prison guards, but Michael's belief in the singularity of prison guards' experiences is noteworthy for its ideological proximity to what Berlet and Lyons call one of the key producerist modes of thinking in modern American populism, which "posits a noble hardworking middle group constantly in conflict with lazy, malevolent, or sinful parasites at the top and the bottom of the social order."[19] One might also trace Michael's desire to "make something" to an early American producerism with roots in the populist movement in the United States. McMath and Foner note that the use of "producerist" rhetoric in populist revolt in the United States in the late nineteenth century stood for a vision of the world the populists would like to see created and was "based on the simple idea that the producer deserves the fruits of his or her work. Put another way, labor creates value."[20] Having a connection to one's work is a central part of Marx's critique of capital: that the process of selling one's labor power creates a condition of alienation. This lack of making or doing productive work sometimes emerges in the idea—for those not employed as guards—that being a prison guard is an easy job for lazy people.

During my fieldwork, I traveled fifteen miles out of the city to conduct an interview with Jamie Mitchell, who worked as a counselor at the ECF. Jamie had moved further into the county, he said, when he sensed that there were many former prisoners moving into Elmira, making the city less safe. Presuming that a more pervasive "law and order" mentality or even a sense of brotherhood with guards might give him a greater sense of safety, I asked Jamie if having such a great density of prison guards living in the city of Elmira had made him feel any safer. He quipped, "You must not know a lot of prison guards." He knew many prison guards, he said, including family members, and said it was mostly a "foot-up job," in which they "sit around and drink coffee and watch guys play basketball." I regularly heard correction officers described as "babysitters for New York State," a way of demeaning the work and simultaneously infantilizing the prisoners.

While police officers are often lauded as heroes, prison guards do not garner the same social status. The stereotype of guards as brutes is quite familiar to Jack Johnson, a defense attorney in Elmira who oversees criminal cases against prison guards when they are tried in the Elmira courts for crimes they are alleged to have committed in the prisons. Johnson reported that even in a prison town, juries frequently sided with prisoners. Noting that images in popular media were not kind to guards, Johnson said, "I don't think people realize it, if you look at our popular culture, every movie, TV show, and anything that's ever set in a prison setting, the inmate is the good guy and the guard is the bad guy, and that is in the back of people's heads." Johnson offered as evidence of this reputation the high number of cases where Chemung County juries vote in favor of an incarcerated defendant against a guard—which he estimated at roughly 50 percent.

In general, I found that the work of the prison leaks out into the prison town through neighbors and family members who bring their jobs home. There is, of course, no uniform idea about guards and their comportment in Elmira, but many of the civilians I spoke with shared the idea that working in prison warped a person's sense of humanity. This connection of prison guards to the brutish conditions of prisons, and particularly guards' enactment of this brutality, seems to be one source of the "misunderstanding" that correction officers described experiencing.

Stacey's study of home health care aides shows that this group of workers found dignity in poorly paid and stigmatized work through their pride in caring for and creating affective bonds with their homebound patients. While being a prison guard is a similarly "dirty job" in that guards are managing people's most basic human functions, unlike home health care aides, prison guards face the consequences both from other COs and from bosses if they attempt or allow bonds with prisoners.[21] As Phillip relayed above, keeping an emotional separation from prisoners is the key to being a prison guard. Two recent productions, Ava Duvarnay's *When They See Us* and the Showtime miniseries *Escape at Dannemora*, highlight the austere way that this "care" is meted out by security staff.[22] In their analysis of *Escape at Dannemora*, Jack Norton and Jared Shanahan highlighted the risk of making human connections in prison: "Against the crushing pressure of bureaucracy, prisoners and staff alike attempt to wrest a little bit of dignity and human connection out of soul-crushing jobs and dehumanizing relationships rooted in brutality, racism, and fear."[23] In *When They See Us*, Duvarnay depicts a scene in which Korey Wise is welcomed upstate with a life-threatening assault by a guard; in a scene years later, while in solitary confinement, Wise receives gifts of a Chia Pet and books from a guard who shows him minimal empathy and calls him "kid." There is no dignity garnered from the prison work, but one can hear Phillip's refrain describing the benefits of being a guard where the pride in one's work is paltry: "Go to someplace with a GED, yeah after seven years I'd like to be making$ 60,000 with six weeks paid vacation, 50 percent pension in twenty-five years and kick-ass medical benefits." For Phillip and others, this was a clear trade for the better.

Despite these benefits, even leaving aside external stigma, the prison guards simply find the work miserable. In 2002, journalist Ted Conover published *Newjack: Guarding Sing Sing*, based on his yearlong experience working as a prison guard at the Sing Sing Correctional Facility in Westchester County, thirty miles north of New York City.[24] I asked a few prison workers—both guards and civilian workers—their opinion of the book: most men had a negative opinion, but only one guard, Phillip, had actually read it. (Based on my data, I believe that Conover provides an accurate account of the life of a guard.) While Phillip enjoyed the history sections of the book, he explained that the book was "bullshit" and that there was no way that Conover could understand what it was like to be a prison guard after having worked only one year.

> He knew what he was doing. He was going to do this for a year and get out. Well, great. You know. Going to the job when you got twenty-four more years to go of doing this.
>
> Yeah, I could do that. It'd be a hell of a lot easier to do. He didn't have that hanging over him. Where there is no light at the end of the tunnel. You're a newjack. All of the jobs are done by seniority. You're gonna have a shit job—a place like Elmira you're gonna have a shit job for like ten or fifteen years because there's so much seniority. And you're just waiting for your raises and then . . . You know, just to the everyday drudgery of, Christ, I gotta do this for eighteen more years. I got six years on the job, but I got eighteen more years, nineteen more years, whatever. He didn't have that. So, to me, he couldn't accurately depict what it's like to be a prison guard. When you got a year on the job—yeah, he had a year on the job, but he had eight months on the job, he's got four months to go. Gee, (laughs), how about having eight months on the job and having four months and twenty-four years to go? Then, tell me how you feel.

Phillip had objections to the book, but his primary concern manifests itself in the book's inability to capture the drudgery and boredom of a life spent working in the prison. Like many civil service jobs, Department of Correctional Services workers earn a pension after twenty-five years of service. Phillip's sense of entrapment reflects both the cost and the benefit of civil service work. Unlike most industries in the United States, work in the government "industries" generally means steady work that can be relied upon as a career. This reflects a national pattern of unionization: 34 percent of U.S. public sector workers are unionized as opposed to 6.4 percent of workers in private industries.[25] The seniority system keeps workers focused on the "better" jobs that lie ahead—better hours, better days off, and better working conditions (in corrections workers tend to associate better jobs with less contact with prisoners). Faced with the economic pressures of raising families, this is a job where, in the words of one CO, "ten years becomes fifteen" and workers become accustomed to higher salaries and reliable health care. Like many prison workers, Phillip paralleled his own work in the prison with the "bids," or prison sentences, of the men incarcerated at Elmira. Phillip called it "doing zero to eight," referring to working his eight hours a day using the common phrasing for prison sentences among incarcerated people, for example "doing a four to six." Gordon Gaughan, told me he was doing twenty-five to life, eight hours at a time. It was not uncommon for my interlocutors to talk about the amount of time they would spend in the prison over the course of their time in corrections and point out that they would spend a third of their lives in the jail.

Finally, the shame of the job of correction officer has its limits or may be particular to some workers. Indeed, it seems that in some circles being a correction officer is a position of relative honor. To begin, despite Gordon's and Phillip's disdain for wearing the uniform in public, I did on occasion see correction officers out in their uniforms—including at Christmas mass at a working-class Roman Catholic church on Elmira's Southside. A young man with a blond buzz cut, perhaps in his late twenties, sat in the row next to my family with his wife or girlfriend, presumably on his way to or from work. On the Southside, a working-class part of town that has been impoverished by the process of economic restructuring, having a "good job" as a correction officer could mean a relative social and economic position of privilege to the many people living on meager seasonal wages, working in retail, or relying on public assistance. For white COs who come from low-income families, becoming a prison guard allows entry into the presumptions of whiteness; that is, the image of how people designated as white should live. This racialization masks the vast differences in class experience guards and other white workers had experienced prior to their employment as a guard. Furthermore, there are men who work as correction officers who volunteer as school coaches, sit on the boards of the Catholic schools, and participate in church volunteering, all positions with a degree of moral authority in the community. Again, we see the work of prison guard as a force of racialization for guards.

When considering how racializations work in the prison, it is essential to consider guards as individuals, as part of a brotherhood of guards, but always as backed up by the arsenal of guns and cages created by the state. As individuals, guards make individual choices within this larger system of control. Although there is some amount of leeway in how guards interpret the work of "care, custody, and control" of prisoners, ultimately their work is to maintain physical control over the inmates at the direction of the state. In her ethnography of an Oregon Special Housing Unit prison, Lorna Rhodes's interlocutor describes himself as a "dog on a chain" for the state, his ability to physically dominate other men unleashed when the state deems it necessary.[26] I find this role of "dog on a chain for the state" as a compelling explanation for why many prison guards experience an ambivalent relationship to the work of controlling other people.

Correction officers sometimes expressed an understanding or identification with the larger social problems faced by the incarcerated men that they guarded. Phillip had worked in sales and attended a few semesters of college before becoming a guard after the arrival of his third child. Phillip, who had an easygoing demeanor and a good sense of humor, shared:

> You know, and you kind of feel bad for them, growing up down there in the city. Or I guess any of the cities now, Albany, Rochester, Syracuse, Buffalo . . . you get the bad sections. But I guess all it takes is somebody gettin' out of there for somebody to say, well if they can do it, then anybody can do it. You chose not to. You chose this. You chose this path in your life. You could have buckled down and studied. Done the right thing. Colin Powell. He came from the South Bronx, didn't he?
>
> I interjected, "But, certainly a lot of them had a lot harder time than I did."

A CAREER YOU CAN COUNT ON!

If you want a job with a future, think about becoming a New York State Correction Officer.
Immediate job openings are available.

The New York State Civil Service exam is being held on November 6th.

HERE'S WHAT YOU GET:
- $12,920/year while training. $13,654 after 6 months. $18,376 after one year.
- Health, dental, prescription drug, life insurance, and retirement benefits.
- More than 2 weeks paid vacation after one year.
- Tuition reimbursement for higher education.
- Continuous on-the-job training to increase your opportunities for promotion.

If you participated in the New York State Civil Service Correction Officer examination in May 1982, you are NOT eligible to take the Correction Officer exam being held on November 6th. There are no minimum qualifications to take the test. However, a high school diploma or equivalent is required for appointment.

EXAM APPLICATIONS MUST BE POSTMARKED BY OCTOBER 4th.
So hurry! For details and an application form,
Call TOLL FREE: **1-800-342-3357**

An Equal Opportunity Employer

A Career in Corrections

THOMAS A. COUGHLIN III
COMMISSIONER
STATE OF NEW YORK
DEPARTMENT OF CORRECTIONAL SERVICES

FIG. 5. "A career you can count on!" Promotional materials from the Department of Corrections about upcoming exams. Department of Corrections, 1982.

He said emphatically, "Oh yeah, but you're not gonna get any sympathy from prison guards."

"Why not?" I asked.

Phillip answered crisply: "Because that would probably humanize the inmates. It would make you seem weaker." In his understanding, distancing oneself from the prisoners is a necessary part of the job. The massive expansion of prisons into Upstate New York and the related

FIG. 6. Memorial to workers at Elmira Correctional Facility. Photo by the author.

recruitment of largely white men from rural areas of the state relies on this articulation of differences, experienced in both material and affective ways. Prison guards imagine themselves as racialized agents of the state; simultaneously, the management of the prison relies significantly on the racializations of jailer and jailed to do the work of social control.

4   Policing the Carceral State

In 2004, a Chemung County legislator began voicing his concerns in public meetings about the county's growing Medicaid budget. The county had become increasingly cash-strapped, and he was convinced that the area had become a magnet for prison families—in his mind, interlopers from other parts of the state in search of good social services. In a pattern common across the American Rust Belt, Elmira had welcomed a new prison with its promise of economic development. A generation later, a panic spread about the families of prisoners expanding the city's welfare benefits and causing crime. Cheryl Walker, a career social worker, grew tired of hearing rumors that the families of inmates at Elmira' s two state prisons were moving to Elmira to commit crimes and collect undeserved welfare benefits. She embarked on what she called an informal research project to determine how many people were moving to Elmira from New York City, Rochester, and Buffalo, cities where large numbers of prisoners come from and, not coincidentally, cities with the state's largest Black populations. Walker said that the county legislator's presumptions were common in Elmira: "I hear from time to time in my travels around the community, 'Oh, those people moved in from New York City, Rochester, and Buffalo. And I have, with some frequency, heard people try to connect the dots between people coming out of the city because their loved one, significant other, whatever, happens to be residing in one of our prisons."

Walker thought that if there were large numbers of people moving to Elmira from New York City, then perhaps the rumors were true. However, when she asked fellow case workers to look at all the new applications coming into the welfare department and ask people where they were moving from if there was not a previous address listed on the application, she found no dominant pattern of migration. "There was no pattern. We had people from all different states. If you looked at states, maybe more from Pennsylvania than other states. But I mean, the number was so small that it was just, you know, not significant." Census data seem to confirm Walker's analysis.[1] While there exists a very small flow of migration into (and an overall outmigration from) Chemung County, the largest group of in-migrants comprised white non-Hispanics from neighboring rural counties.[2] Taken together, this suggests a pattern of white rural movement across Upstate and not an influx of Black residents to Elmira. Despite this lack of a larger pattern of migration, the fact that anyone had moved to Chemung County to be near a loved one in prison was an anecdote with powerful ramifications, according to Walker.

In this chapter, I draw on the Birmingham cultural studies tradition of combining ethnographic and historical methods to understand the broader context of crime. Reflecting on *Policing the Crisis* on its thirtieth anniversary, Hall et al. wrote that while they were influenced by sociology and critical criminology, "the overarching object of analysis in PTC was not 'crime' or even 'society', but the 'social formation,' conceptualized as an ensemble of practices, institutions, forces, and contradictions."[3] In other words, in order to understand the heightened attention to "mugging" in 1980s Birmingham, England, one must understand the history of the people living there and how they worked, organized their families, and went about their everyday lives. In bringing this lens to the study of crime in Elmira, I necessarily begin with the idea that the institutional violence of the prison leaks into the everyday policing of people outside of the prison; crime therefore must be viewed with a wider lens than simply deviant acts of an individual. In this chapter, I use the term "panic" to describe, as Hall et al. did, "excessive waves of fear and apprehension amongst sections of the public about a perceived threat to society itself."[4] In doing so, I highlight how the massive carceral infrastructure in Elmira exacerbates racialized criminalization.

In Elmira, the thread of panic that former prisoners—and, more often in the last two decades, the families of prisoners—are moving to Elmira and causing an increase in crime merits further scrutiny. There is significant movement of people into and out of the Elmira Correctional Facility every day: workers, visitors, prisoners as they are released, moved, and reclassified. There is also movement of ideas, goods, and materials. But the panic taking hold in Elmira has little to do with these mundane elements of containment and more with systemic containment of racialized groups, in particular the containment of Blackness. The panic blends two of the strongest threads of anti-Black racism in the United States, painting all prisoners as Black and all Black Americans as welfare cheats and criminals; these ideas enmesh with the larger national race and crime panic that has been developing since at least the War on Drugs in the early 1970s. But perhaps most importantly, the panic is everywhere: at a yoga class, repeated by concerned advocates who had heard the whispers at the church soup kitchen, in the newspaper, and in courtrooms, people postulate that former prisoners and the families of prisoners are the source of Elmira's problems.

The panic's roots in fears of Black migration, criminality, and welfare dependency reflects larger tropes of racial order with roots as far back as the system of American slavery, but the new economy has created new fault lines for the racialization of poor and working-class people through the carceral state. The post-Fordist period is marked by the flexibility of processes of accumulation and the shift of economic and social risk onto the working classes; we are less likely to make decent wages, to be protected by unions, and to be able to own a home. These new patterns of production and new forms of dispossession are coupled with a reordering of racial inequalities; the expansion of the carceral state is an essential architecture of racial difference in the post-Fordist period.

The City of Elmira is 75 percent white, 15 percent Black, 5 percent mixed race, and less than 5 percent Latino/a/x.[5] Unlike the fictive image of an all-white "small town America" that circulates in the United States, Elmira has been home to a sizeable African American population, between 2 and 10 percent of the total population of the city, since 1850. Dozens of Black men and women were recorded as being held as slaves in the 1820s and the city was home to an African Methodist Episcopal Church that opened its doors in 1841.[6] Since the 1860s, a Black enclave in Elmira's East Side, at that time called "Slabtown," has been home to many Black-owned businesses and churches. Some residents were formerly enslaved men and women who settled in the neighborhood after reaching Elmira via the Underground Railroad.[7] But the shifting boundaries of Elmira's Black neighborhoods suggest a possible source of the panic following a period of prison expansion in Elmira. The east side of the city underwent profound changes during urban renewal in the 1970s, when many parts of the neighborhood were bulldozed for the purpose of building a "parkway" through the center of town—a boulevard commonly known as the "road to nowhere." Since the 1970s, on account of the loss of population as factories closed, and perhaps also because of dislocations from urban renewal and/or due to somewhat of a relaxing of historical spatial segregation (different Elmirans suggested both), there has been some movement of Elmira's African American population out of the east side and into downtown and the Southside. During this period, the racial demographics of Elmira remained stable, but the geography of segregation became somewhat more relaxed in working-class neighborhoods; that is, the percentage of the population of Elmira that is Black and white has remained the same in the city of Elmira since shortly after World War II, but African Americans have moved into traditionally white working-class neighborhoods in larger numbers.

"Connecting the Dots"

Jim Pfeiffer, a local journalist who wrote a weekly, often humorous column in the local *Star-Gazette*, published a front-page article titled "Blame It on the Prisons?" shortly before I moved back to Elmira to do my field research.[8] Pfeiffer interviewed a former chaplain at the ECF, a social service worker, a man formerly incarcerated from the ECF who lives in Elmira, the chief of police, and a criminal court judge to get at the heart of the question on the minds of many Elmirans: *Is it true that the prisons are responsible for the crimes?* In Pfeiffer's article, only the chief of police and a criminal court judge considered former inmates settling in Elmira to be a problem that warranted inquiry and suspicion. On the contrary, the Department of Correctional Services media relations officer cited the fact that inmates are transferred quite often as a reason that, logically, families of inmates would not settle in Elmira. (Of course, it is in the interest of the Department of Correctional Services, for the purposes of future prison siting and general maintenance, to convey the message to prison towns that prisons are so well contained and policed that they are spaces separate from the city or town where they are located.) Pfeiffer's article is sandwiched in between articles on recent crimes and the police response to the sale and distribution of crack cocaine in the area, written from the perspective of the police. In the end, Pfeiffer concluded that "it probably happens, but not as often as most people believe." This is the same general conclusion I came to after my fieldwork, but the question remains: Why is this "anecdote," as so many of my interlocutors called it, so powerful?[9]

A June 18, 2021, Facebook post by local news station WENY.com titled "My Twin Tiers," reported that five officers were injured during a fight at the prison. A respondent wrote, "I wish they would close that prison. I feel bad saying that because I know it employs a lot of people but it also brings in all the trash for the cities so they can be closer to their baby daddies."[10] A woman commented on his post, "It doesn't need to close, just need tighter control on what's allowed in. If they stop offering free rides to visitors, the trash wouldn't be here."[11] There is significant debate on the thread—after all it is the internet—but this dynamic of tracing any crime to the prison is part and parcel of the porous prison.

The discursive function of "connecting the dots"—in Walker's words—between the prison and quotidian life outside of the prison gates marks an important way in which prisons and the carceral work of policing that extends beyond their walls heighten the criminalization of Black life in the United States. The carceral state wields the authority to both criminalize and normalize, marking Black Americans as suspect and simultaneously obscuring the history of Black Elmira and rendering people outsiders in their own places. The very American racial anxieties creating a fictitious criminality and welfare dependency become projected onto a captive population but spill out beyond the walls of the prison.

It is clear there are Elmirans who visit their loved ones or friends at the ECF, and it is equally clear that families of incarcerated men and women are not moving to Elmira in any large numbers. Yet, the idea that there is a relationship between Black incarcerated men on the one hand and crime and welfare dependency among Black people in Elmira on the other remains a powerful discursive practice. The particular virulent discourse that I focus on here—"let's tear down the prisons so that the welfare families go somewhere else"—couples the fear of crime with animosity for the racialized poor. While analyzing the statistical insignificance of this group in relationship to the larger population of Elmira, I seek to think through what it is imagined that this group of people do once they get here and "settle."

The power of this idea—prisoners' families are coming here and living in our city!—stems from its enactment in and through the carceral state; it has found clear support among the city's elite. Elmira City Chief of Police W. Scott Drake told Pfeiffer of the theory that prisons cause crime, "I think it's true . . . But there's no way to measure it. Not all the families of the inmates are bad people, but some of them are no better than the inmates, and one bad family can cause a lot of havoc in the community."[12] In an observation of criminal court proceedings in 2008, I saw one judge ask numerous defendants if they were from Elmira. He asked a Black defendant, "What brings you to the area?" In a context where the head of the Elmira Police Department believes that his police force is policing the families of prisoners at a maximum-security prison who are often "no better than the inmates," the police are defining the problem of crime as related to an already marked population of "ex-convicts." Elmira's population lives with high levels of underemployment, and the regional displacements from gentrifying New York City, Rochester, and Syracuse are coming home to roost in the city to some extent. But certainly, Elmira is not the haven for the poor and families of incarcerated men with fruitful access to social services that many people fantasize it to be.

Policing Black Elmira

The Elmira Police Department polices the city with a very racialized notion that prisoners don't belong in Elmira and must be contained. In summer 2007 twenty-one people were arrested for various federal- and state-level drug trafficking crimes—ten African American men, seven African American women, one white man, and one white woman—under the umbrella of "Operation Crack Hammer." The mug shots of these defendants were shown innumerable times on the television news and were printed together in the front section of the newspaper, accompanied by a quote in the adjacent story from the chief of police: "I don't think any of them were born in Elmira. They have no vested interest here."[13] In one of the strings of arrests as a part of this operation, heralded by the Elmira Police Department as making a major "dent" in local drug trafficking, five people were charged with crimes.[14] These included one twenty-seven-year-old man who was charged with third-degree possession (for being caught with the smallest amount of a controlled substance to constitute a crime) of cocaine, and four others, including two seventeen-year-olds and an eighteen-year-old, who were charged with loitering and misdemeanor counts of marijuana possession. These charges indicate that the arrests were hardly a takedown of high-level drug traffickers.[15] One local businessman, John Cooke, a white man involved in civil rights issues, saw this newspaper story as one of the most damaging and racist occurrences in recent Elmira history. As he saw it, the usage of a series of mug shots along with police bravado surrounding the arrest of the men and women was unprecedented. Indeed, a few days after the story ran, I was fifty miles away chatting with a cousin's neighbor, who mentioned that he saw "Elmira was having a lot of problems with drugs"—a direct result of the story. The criminalization and media hype of Elmira's "Drug War" suggest that despite Black Elmira's hundreds of years of history, African Americans can swiftly be determined to be "not from here" by association with the carceral state.

During my fieldwork, I met two men who were raised in other parts of New York State and stayed in Elmira after their incarceration following their release from the ECF. While I found that the numbers of incarcerated people returning to Elmira was not the tidal wave of dependency imagined in the panic, it is nonetheless not surprising that a few former prisoners have relied on social networks they made during their incarceration and chose to remain. Prison visits are all too infrequent in state prisons. Analysis by the Prison Policy Initiative of Bureau of Justice Statistics showed that 30 percent of prisoners in state prisons had received a visit in a typical month.[16] Particularly for people who have served long sentences in prison, the social and emotional toll of prison, the lack of affordable housing upon release, and the discrimination in employment based on felony convictions often leave formerly incarcerated people without a place to go. If one does have a personal connection to Elmira, moving to this small city may understandably be the best choice for some of them.

As has already been established, for some white Elmirans, the reduction and geographic reorganization of manufacturing work over the course of the 1970s and '80s led the loss of stable, relatively well-paid work and the access it provided to homeownership and status, which has translated into a larger feeling of loss and a scapegoating of Black Americans as responsible for it. In the presence of the prison as an employer and the dearth of left-wing social movements, many Elmirans, and indeed, many white working-class people, rely on the explanatory framework of criminality and moral inferiority to make sense of everyday life in both the prison town and the prison. Many prison workers feel they are at the mercy of both the prisoners, whom they see as having an expanded repertoire of rights, and the bosses at the Department of Corrections and Community Supervision who control the conditions of their working lives.[17] Following this distorted logic, there is no location for them other than between these two groups. Prison work provides the architecture of such a world view—it makes visible and "true" the hierarchies of race and class as the "anecdotes" tell them.

The pattern of economic restructuring and resulting impoverishment is not specific to Elmira but reflective of national shifts in the political economy of cities.[18] Cities close to Elmira, like Binghamton, Rochester, and Wilkes-Barre/Scranton, Pennsylvania, in addition to bigger cities like Detroit and Philadelphia, mirror the pattern of economic restructuring and shifting racial geographies that played out in Elmira. As high-paying manufacturing jobs left—many organized around the Fordist model of manufacturing—many people left the city of Elmira catalyzing a spiral downward of housing values on the historically white working-class Southside of Elmira and in the city center. This shift created new housing opportunities for poor Blacks and poor whites who moved to the area in larger numbers from a variety of locations in the surrounding area. As such, rather than reflecting a reality of high crime committed by "outside" Black people, my ethnographic work indicates that the panic focuses on the mundane criminalization of ordinary Black life.

Policing Black Life

Marco Roy, a middle-aged African American man, had met his girlfriend when she visited Roy's friend at the prison. She visited him frequently while he was in prison. When he was released, he returned home to the Bronx before coming back to Elmira to be with his girlfriend, and has lived in the city for ten years. Roy argued that men incarcerated in Elmira's prisons very rarely settle in Elmira upon release. "It's a myth," he said. According to Roy, people accustomed to city life saw Elmira as "so spooky, it's so quiet, it's too scary"; indeed, among prisoners the prevailing image of Elmira was of a "hick town" full of "rednecks." As already indicated, DOCS manipulates this cultural difference by using the distance from family and the rurality of the prison as an additional aspect of punishment for men from the New York City metropolitan area. Unsurprisingly, my research found that for many families of incarcerated people, their loved ones aren't interested in living in Elmira when they are released from prison.

Roy encountered some problems with the police when he first moved to Elmira ("because I drove a nice car," he said) but now felt that the police left him alone because they were familiar with him. He described a few encounters with correction officers he had known in the prison, none of which he described as particularly confrontational. One encounter was with a CO he considered "fruity" or effeminate. While relaying the story to me, he described to me mocking this CO's sexuality while he was in prison. However, when they saw one another at a local sandwich shop, Roy describes it as a casual, uneventful meeting: "I go in there and I say, 'Fruity, is that you?' He turns around and he says, 'Hey what you doin' up here?' I was like, 'What you mean what I'm doing up here'. And he says, 'Ain't you from New York?' I was like, 'Yeah, I got a girlfriend up here and I'm just working.' So he said, 'You stayin' out of trouble?' And I was like, 'Yeah I'm staying out of trouble. You know, working, doing my regular thing, my routine.' But that was it basically." Roy's narrative of his encounters with guards echoes descriptions by guards of similar encounters.

Dennis Hardy, a criminal defense lawyer who regularly represents clients incarcerated at the Elmira and Southport Correctional Facility and poor Elmirans in criminal court, found the idea that former inmates and their families are moving to Elmira "absurd":

People say this all the time, and again, being one who represents prisoners and who represents poor people generally that are charged with crimes, I can't think of a single instance, and I mean this sincerely, where somebody's moved here, that I'm aware of, to be closer to their incarcerated family member. People allege this all the time, and it may happen, but I can't think of a single instance of that. And I think the reality is that there's such a big cultural difference from where these people come from in New York City and then moving up here to be close to an inmate, I think they'd have a tough time.

When I asked if he thought the erroneous perception was fed by discussions of crime in the local paper, where it is often noted when a defendant is from New York City or other parts of the state, he said, "Oh, yeah, and people just assume it's the incarcerated family member that brought them here." A menacing triumvirate—race, urbanity, and dependency—emerges in these exchanges making and remaking the racialized carceral state on the outside of the prison.

There is some indication that African Americans are moving to Elmira for reasons unrelated to the prison. Dawn Stevens, an African American woman in her forties, moved to Elmira from Jamaica, Queens, New York City in 1999 with her husband and young son. Dawn was in search of a cheaper cost of living and an escape from the guns and drugs of her old neighborhood. Because she had always worked in financial services, a nearly nonexistent industry in Elmira, she said finding work was one of the most difficult aspects of her move. When we spoke at her home, a modernly decorated apartment on the Southside of Elmira, she listed the things she liked and disliked about living in Elmira:

> The cost of living is lower. When I lived in the city, the whole time I lived in the city—well, you know, you've got trains, you got buses, and you don't have to drive anywhere. I never had a car in my life. Never had to. Since I've been up here, I've had two [cars]. I like that. What I don't like is the fact that jobs are scarce. I don't like the fact that there is nothing for youth. There's nothing for the kids here, which is probably why kids get into all kinds of mischief. What else are they going to do?

Dawn describes the challenges of urban life, big and small:

> I left the city because there was a lot of—you know, there was crime increasing and there was this and that, and I never felt afraid walking

up and down the street, or coming home from a club, 1:00 or 2:00 a.m. riding the subway; I was never afraid of that type of thing. But when you get to the point where you gotta look over your shoulders to go to the store, your kids can't go outside and play, that kind of stuff, then it's time to leave because you're living in a prison. You're living in a prison. So I came up here to get away from that, so if you're reading in the newspapers about, oh, well, there's shooting over here, this one got shot, and there's big drug dealers here, I'm like, wait a minute, didn't I come up here to get away from that stuff?

Dawn shared with some other Elmirans some concern over the possible increased violence because of the prison. Despite her concern over the violence, which she also believed the media "went after" in search of a good story, Dawn liked her new city and her work in social services. When I asked her if her son experienced more police scrutiny in Elmira than white teenagers, Dawn said that although she did not subscribe to a "whitey's holding us down" attitude, she did believe that her son was more scrutinized by the police. She noted she had told him, "Not to do a little bit of anything" because "you're the first person they're going to look at if something stupid happens."

Similarly, Reverend Ruben Johnson and his wife, Betty Johnson, were concerned that Black men were being racially profiled in Elmira. The Reverend Johnson, the pastor at an African American church, said that undoubtedly at "one point" in the 1980s there were higher numbers of young men coming out of the prison and staying in Elmira, a pattern he saw continuing today to a lesser extent. "I knew these guys personally," he added. Reverend Johnson and Mrs. Johnson were not concerned that these men would bring more crime to the area. They attributed the crime to drugs and a need to find income to survive. They were, however, concerned that the local police and DOCS would do "anything in their power" to keep the ex-prisoners out of Elmira. Mrs. Johnson added, "Well, there are people that don't want us on the street. And we're not in prison." For the Johnson family, the fear of prison families was very clearly connected to anti-Black racism; rather than a fear of crime, they see anti-prison sentiment as a reflection of a desire to make all Black people—prisoners and free—unwelcome in Elmira.

Visiting the Carceral City

Despite the low numbers of prisoners receiving visits from loved ones, the visiting room is an essential point of intervention for families. "Without the affective-political labor of these anonymous women," anthropologist Orisanmi Burton writes, "hundreds of thousands of incarcerated people would be crushed under the weight of the carceral empire."[19] Because the visiting room serves as a site of care and connection to home, it remains a point of anxiety and concern for guards and for some Elmirans. The small number of Elmirans who visit their incarcerated kin at the prison relative to the larger population of Elmira is important, but it is equally crucial to analyze what it is imagined that this group of people do once they get here and "settle." Moreover, rather than envisioning the prison as a magnet for poor African Americans and Latinos from New York State's major cities—the imagined and feared "families"—we should understand the Elmira and Southport Correctional Facilities and the carceral state more generally as contributing to the general dislocation of poor people of color throughout New York State. Due to the large numbers of people incarcerated, the prison has become part of the orbit of social life of poor Elmirans and poor New Yorkers, a quotidian experience of dislocation and dispossession that is at the crux of carceral state-making.[20]

It is New York State policy for men and women to be paroled to the county in which they are arrested; every person sent to state prison by a Chemung County criminal court judge will thus be released to the city of Elmira. More concretely, if a man lived in Buffalo in Erie County but was arrested for an assault in Elmira, he would be paroled to the city of Elmira. This reduces the likelihood that prison release is a direct conduit for the movement of families of prisoners, as many prisoners would be obligated to move to other counties upon parole. According to the local homeless shelter, in one month in 2007 three men and one woman, all of whom were former Elmira residents, wrote requesting housing upon their release from prisons in other parts of Upstate New York. The county received thirty-eight total similar referrals in 2007, as a result of the described state policy.[21]

The geographic distribution of visits to the ECF sheds some further light on whether there are families of prisoners living in Elmira. Based on an analysis of records kept by the visitor's center, there are on average of ten visits each weekend day from local people to the prison. For example, the visitor's center was open ten days in March 2007 over five weekends. Nine hundred and nine people visited 596 prisoners that month. That is an average of 140 total visits (often more than one person is visiting one prisoner, so it counts as one visit) per weekend to a facility housing 1800 men, an indication that fewer than 10 percent of incarcerated men got a visit on any given weekend. It is highly likely, too, that individual men are getting repeat visits in a single weekend, thus making that number even lower. One weekend in March, eleven local people visited prisoners , including ten women and one man. Three weekends previous there were twenty-nine visits from the Elmira area, including twenty-one women, two men, and six children. In one month in 2005, there were 36 visits from the Jamestown area, 39 from the Utica area, 123 local visitors, and 296 from New York City. It is thus clear, at the very least, that there are Elmirans who have family or friends who are incarcerated at the prison, but the feared families of prisoners are barely a whisper of a presence outside of the visiting room. Notably, DOCS has a general pattern of moving prisoners away from their families; Upstate men and women are incarcerated in other parts of Upstate or downstate, and men and women from New York City, who make up the overwhelming majority of the state's prison population, are generally incarcerated in prisons upstate.[22] Because of this general pattern of placing prisoners far from their homes, it is possible to extrapolate that there might be a small number of people who have moved to Elmira to be closer to a man incarcerated at the ECF. However, it is also clear that these numbers are quite low, considering that there are on average twenty visitors per weekend, including children. In a county of over ninety thousand people (and this analysis counted an even larger swath of surrounding rural areas as "local"), this is a small number.[23]

There was some debate among my interlocutors about whether this data misrepresents visiting patterns because the numbers only cover visits that occurred on weekends, when the visitor's center is open. One individual said that local people tended to visit during the week after work because they wanted to beat the weekend crowds. On the weekends, because there are limited numbers of visits that can occur simultaneously, visits can be "terminated"—to use the Department of Corrections and Community Supervision's language—if there is deemed to be not enough time. In the event of a crowded visiting room, visits from local people will get bumped if the guards know that the visitor can easily return. Another frequent visitor said the opposite was true—a person might work during the week and therefore visit on the weekends, possibly visiting both days. I did not have access to data about how many visitors are coming to see kin, a lover, or a friend, versus local religious people on missionary visits. (One of my interlocutors met her currently incarcerated husband on such a religious visit). Thirdly and finally, it is unclear whether the incarcerated men receiving visits are from the Elmira area originally, as opposed to the group that populates the panicked racial imaginaries of some locals—"outsiders."

Building the Carceral State Count by Count

Having heard stories from guards about seeing men they had known during their incarceration at the grocery store, at the mall, and at high school basketball games, I became interested in the extent to which guards view themselves as still "on duty" when they are on the streets of Elmira. Similar to police, guards often describe hypervigilance in social settings outside of work, for example, never sitting with one's back to the door or sensing in a crowd when there is a fight brewing. How does this vigilance translate to guards' experience living in a prison town? I received incredibly varied responses from prison workers regarding the presence of men formerly incarcerated at the ECF on the streets of the city of Elmira, a set of viewpoints that may be linked to my interlocutors' views of incarcerated men more generally. It seems that those prison workers who considered incarcerated men "low-lifes" were more likely to see former prisoners having a negative impact on the civic and social life of Elmira and offer more stories about negative encounters. Gordon Gaughan, the career correction officer introduced in an earlier chapter, described an encounter that he viewed as particularly distressing:

> I remember one time it was Sunday, Palm Sunday. I was going to St. Savior's Church with my wife and my two kids. And the priest was

right up on the front there greeting people as they came in. As we were coming in . . . across the way there's a convenient store and there was two ex-convicts there. And across the street they yell to me, "Hey you fucking pig." Can you believe this? Palm Sunday, I'm going to church, and they yell this across the street. And I looked at my wife, and I said, who's yelling like that? And my wife she goes like that, [points], and I looked over and I recognized them right away and they're laughin'. So, I went into the church, used the phone and called the police and had them charged for harassment.

When Gordon relayed this story to me it was clear that this was not a common exchange; rather, this rare encounter was disruptive to his experience of living in Elmira. For the most part, Gordon had been able to shield his family from what he saw as the "grotesque" world of the prison.

In the background of this narrative lies the day-to-day policing of the prison. When Gordon, a law enforcement officer for the state, called the local police they respected his role as a law enforcement official and arrested the young men. In another situation, it is possible that this would be considered a minor infraction, something in which it would be unnecessary to involve the police. In the case of police, Micol Seigel calls the quotidian work of policing doing "violence work"—"making real" the state in the everyday.[24] In this case, the hierarchical relationships formed in and by the prison between prisoner and guard, Black and white, police and policed, are then replicated on the streets of Elmira, and Gaughan serves a role as a representative and a bit part architect of the carceral state.

In an opposing narrative, Keith Rollins, a bespectacled white-haired, civilian worker, a self-described "white liberal" who spoke respectfully about incarcerated men, looked surprised when I asked him if he had ever encountered someone he knew from the "inside" on the streets of Elmira. Rollins said he had never seen anyone whom he knew to be incarcerated at Elmira outside the prison. After thinking for a minute, he corrected himself to say that once he had run into a former inmate on the streets of downtown Corning, New York, a town about twenty miles east. The man was a native of the area and returned there after getting out of prison. They shook hands and the man thanked him for his help while he was in prison, and they moved on. Rollins had worked at the ECF for twenty-five years.

Despite describing uneventful encounters with former inmates on the streets of Elmira, Greg Shaughnessy, a man retired from thirty-four years as a correction officer, had some anxieties about his prison life bleeding into his home life. Early in his career, on a job transporting inmates, Greg took an inmate from the ECF to a doctor's appointment at St. Joseph's hospital downtown, where inmates regularly receive medical care. Greg described the man, a Native American, as a "Big Indian" and recalled thinking, "Holy creep, he's huge!" According to Greg, the man asked him during the ride in the prison van down a main thoroughfare to the hospital, "You live in this shit town? Well, you can have it." Greg was rattled and vowed never to take an inmate on transportation again. Greg's recounting of the incident and his decision not to do prison work that took him outside of the prison brings together interwoven issues. First, the description of the man's physicality—his largeness a symbol and marker of dominance within the prison and his brownness a racialized marker of "badness," centers Greg's image of the man. The "Big Indian" is set against a backdrop of Greg's own town—a set of power-laden relationships he would rather not, and chose not to, have to deal with outside of the prison.

In a very roundabout way, Greg described how men did their jobs in different ways and that a violent temperament on the job would mean a different experience at home. He repeated to me many times that "the job never bothered me. I never drank from it. I never took drugs from it. None of that. I never—I just never did. I left the job there and when I went home, I was home." He described a recent experience on the streets of Elmira. "In fact, my nephew was up one day and he says, 'hey, uncle', he says. 'The guy's looking at you'. I said, 'What guy?' 'That guy over there.' 'What guy?' This kid came up. 'Hey, how are you doing?' 'Oh, yeah,' I says, [smiling] 'I remember him.'" Greg told me this story in a matter-of-fact tone.

He then returned to the idea that he didn't let the job bother him: "Because if you do something that you're not too proud of, you know, then all of a sudden, well, you've gotta deal with that. And I always tried to be on the up and up. I really did. I didn't hate anybody. I didn't like some of the stuff that I was seeing and hearing, but you know, hey. Everybody gets theirs at the end. That's the bottom line. You're gonna get yours, good, bad, or indifferent, you're gonna get what you've got coming to you."

Building the Carceral State Brick by Brick

Here, I return again to the idea that the prison serves as a scapegoat for impoverishment and resultant anxieties about crime and containment as a force of racialization. In summer 2003 two men chiseled through the ceiling of their top floor cell at the ECF, went through the air ducts, and rappelled down the side of the prison with a string of bed sheets tied together. At this point, the site was one of the few prisons in the state with no perimeter fence, and the men escaped into the woods to the west of the facility. They were captured a few days later just over five miles from the prison.[25] In the weeks following the prison break, then-mayor Stephen Hughes organized a meeting to "bridge the gap" in communications between the prison and local officials. The mayor, the warden, a representative from NYSCOPBA, the police, a city councilman, the city manager, and three unidentified "city residents" all agreed to participate in the group. DOCS for its part underplayed the creation of such a group as an indication of problems, stating that thirty of the seventy facilities in the state also had a sort of community liaison group.[26] The one "concerned resident" quoted in the *Star-Gazette* was the superintendent of the Elmira Heights School District, who expressed her concern that a school located very near to the prison did not hear about the breakout via DOCS, but rather on the radio. However, many other residents were apparently unruffled by the prison break. One neighbor commented that "I think we are living in the safest place, right next to the prison. They're not going to come here for coffee and a cab. They are going to head for the hills."[27]

When I went to the home of Carol Lewis, I was shocked that she lived quite literally in the shadow of the prison. I asked Lewis, a white woman and herself the wife of a prisoner at a medium security prison, if it worried her to live so close to the prison. She wasn't worried, she told me, but the escape had made her children (who lived outside the city) concerned for her safety. Lewis, on the other hand, said she never wanted to leave Elmira. She explained that her low cost of living allowed her to maintain her well-kept home ("I paid $40,000!" she said, "Where else am I going to go to get that?"). A hundred of her friends and neighbors had signed a letter welcoming her husband, who is also white, to the area upon his release. "Nobody seems to pay any attention to the prison, to be perfectly honest with you," added Lewis. While often serving as a lightning rod for the causes of social problems, the day-to-day running of the prison is generally not a controversial aspect of the landscape of Elmira.

The meeting of public officials regarding the prison, which arose from the only prison break in Elmira since 1984 (when two men escaped by way of a garbage truck and were caught soon after), was not mentioned again in the newspaper or in any archival information I had access to. The fact that the prison/town relations committee fizzled out has several likely causes. First, although the ECF (unlike the Southport Correctional Facility, which was on a rural road) is quite centrally located and visible as a part of the city, the day-to-day functioning of the prison (particularly the everyday lives of the men incarcerated there) is out of sight. After the initial concern over the escape, the work of the prison again faded into the mundane daily life of the city. Secondly, it appears that the creation of a panel to deal with concerns was solely a public relations move. While there appeared to be, in this instance, a disconnect between the DOCS high-level bureaucracy and City of Elmira officials, there are many rank-and-file correction officers living in Elmira and Chemung County who have connections to local public officials and would share information with police. Therefore, the presence of a representative of NYSCOPBA and *not* of the New York State Public Employees Federation (PEF), the union of civilian prison workers who are not considered law enforcement, signifies the city's containment-oriented response. This panel's convening solely at a moment of crisis suggests that the prison was not considered any great threat to public safety, in that local government did not need to manage public ideas about the prison on an ongoing basis. While the escape brought the prison into the local (and national) spotlight, the crisis created a problem which quickly faded. Further, this suggests that the panic about the prisoners' families and former prisoners causing crime has very little to do with the ability of the prison to control the prisoners within the

FIG. 7. Photo caption, as printed in the *Star-Gazette*: "Armed Elmira Correctional Facility officers stop traffic around 8:30 [a.m.] Monday on West Water Street in Elmira as they search for two escaped convicts." John P. Cleary, *Elmira Star-Gazette*, July 8, 2007, 1A. Star-Gazette—USA TODAY NETWORK.

prison from escaping but rather reflected the desired containment of the "dangerous classes."

After the escape, the state spent more than $3 million to construct a double perimeter fence around the prison. According to one interlocutor, for years the city had declined to sell the Department of Correctional Services a small piece of land necessary for such a fence to be built, only to be up-in-arms that such a fence would have kept an escape from happening. The fence makes for a dramatically different facade of the prison, which sits on a hill on the northwestern edge of Elmira city but in the middle of a residential neighborhood. After construction, it became part of the ongoing process of carceral state-making—a mechanism through which the image of the prison as separate and prisoners as dangerous is made and remade through the management of crises.

Conclusion

I have shown here that there is a panic in Elmira that the families of prisoners and former prisoners are moving to this small city, committing criminal acts, and collecting undeserved welfare benefits and have argued that this panic must be understood in direct dialogue with the arsenals, walls, and cages that encage a racialized population. If we are truly interested in the abolition of prisons, as many of us who study this system of immiseration are, the prison must be understood not only as an imposing physical infrastructure but as a part of a carceral state that also traffics in ideas: the idea that Black Americans are criminals, don't belong in white spaces, are dependent on the state, and need a harsher degree of social control to be contained. Those ideas and the apparatuses that seek to control them "leak" from the prison, reinventing old hierarchies of race and segregation with a heightened language of criminalization, backed by the institutional power of the prison. The prison, therefore, must be understood in the larger frame of what Roseberry called the "landscape of hegemony." It is in this broader context that the carceral state is realized and in which the carceral state must be undone.

5   Porous Prison

The prison is theorized as set apart from normal life but leaks out of the walls of the institution in big and small ways. As historian of civil rights—era prison organizing Dan Berger has written, "The prison needs to be thought of in the context of movement—if nothing else, the forced migration from home to prison—rather than stasis."[1] In this chapter, I focus on how—despite increasingly intricate barriers of containment—prisoners, guards, visitors, money, consumer goods, food, and disease circulate through the prison and through "free" Elmira. Without losing sight of the arsenal of weapons available to the state to maintain incarceration and the limits to people's freedom, I argue that the prison must be understood as a porous place. Berger shows that it was the political organizing of prisoners during the civil rights era that made space for this porousness; any ounce of capaciousness, any freedom to read, or study, or create and maintain human relationships was a hard-won freedom.[2] This chapter builds on that idea and makes a parallel argument about the porousness of the other scales of life at the prison: between the "inside" and "the outside." As I have described in previous chapters, COs and their families, DOCS officials, and many Elmirans view the prison as a place separate from Elmira. Here, in contrast, I focus on the ways people, money, viruses, and ideas circulate between the prison and the town. I do so via three examples. First, I demonstrate how, at the height of the COVID-19 pandemic and movements for racial and economic justice in the spring and summer of 2020, prison guards and civil staff at the prison served as conduits both for COVID and for the heightened attention to the racial and gender hierarchies of the prison. Second, I describe how through the care of prisoners by their families and small inputs of capital, the prison is a part of the larger picture of Elmira as a place. Finally, I show how prisoners' money, their ideas, and their families move through the city.

Pandemic Prison

Perhaps at no other time in recent history has the ECF been so palpably a part of the narrative of everyday life in Elmira than during the first waves of the COVID-19 pandemic. On October 2, 2020, just months before the arrival of the first vaccines for the virus in the United States, a NYSCOPBA union representatives counted four COVID positive COs and thirty more officers in quarantine from the prison.[3] At this point in the pandemic, the Center for Disease Control and state health officials had a better knowledge of community spread; for example, they were aware that COVID was an airborne disease and that the ventilation of buildings and physical distancing were essential to keep community spread abated, a fact that was less clear when the virus was first discovered in the United States in February 2020. The conditions inside New York State prisons require men to be indoors, sharing cells, on long corridors with dozens of other cells with poor ventilation. Guards walk the same hallways and stand in the same mess halls as the incarcerated men. In the most profoundly biological way, it is impossible for the virus to distinguish between a guard and a prisoner, or a guard and a visitor, making clear the porous boundaries of the prison, making it vulnerable to the risk of viral infection. One of the foundational ideas in epidemiology is the notion of community spread; COVID-19 laid bare that the men incarcerated at the ECF are very much a part of the community of Elmira.

But when the first signs of an uptick in COVID cases appeared in Elmira, NYSCOPBA called for a lockdown on prison visits rather than an increase in masking and other personal protective equipment, arguing that the risk of COVID spread was coming from prison visits. One Republican state senator, Tom O'Mara, and two Republican state assembly members, Phil Palmesano and Chris Friend, followed NYSCOPBA's line and threw down a familiar racial trope: "stop busing visitors from downstate" into the prison as a way to stop COVID.[4] A woman who visits her fiancé in the prison regularly had a different theory, arguing (without giving her name) to the local TV station, "The corrections officers are putting the inmates at risk. They're the ones that are bringing [COVID] in because they don't care about wearing masks there." The news station reported that the visitor "follows all the guidelines and precautions, [and] she claims the staff is not doing the same."[5] Given the low vaccination rate of correction officers in New York State this assertion by a visitor is not without merit. Anonymous complaints were made to the Chemung County Board of Health that staff who were COVID positive were not alerted when another staff member tested positive.[6] Another complaint noted that prisoners were not being isolated in an infirmary once they tested positive.[7] Despite this apparent lack of interest in other health protections by some prison staff, COVID brought a new reasoning for the guards' union to push for a more complete "containment" of prisoners by prison staff: eroding the freedom of movement within the prison, the freedom to get packages and access to materials, and the freedom to receive visits by family members and friends.

Within the first week of the nationwide lockdown, advocates noted that prisons and jails were likely petri dishes of infectious disease and urged state correctional agencies to release sick and aging prisoners.[8] This assertion has proven to be true: according to the *Journal of the American Medical Association*, the death rate of prisoners across the United States from COVID was more than double that of the general U.S. population.[9] Despite clear knowledge of the scope of the threat of COVID in prisons and other "congregate" settings, three weeks later, on October 26, the number of COVID cases at the ECF reached 550, comprising nearly a third of the men incarcerated at the prison. The DOCS spokesperson told media that most of the cases were "asymptomatic."[10] Prisoners and their families, however, noted that this massive outbreak was not coupled with a robust public health response but met with a bleak silence. Following the pattern of the previous decades, prisoners reported receiving nominal care and at the whims of prison staff.

On October 27, 2020, the COVID crisis at the prison drew protestors from all over New York State. Fifty protestors gathered outside the ECF, demanding the release of sick and aging prisoners and the increase of protections for prisoners.[11] Some of the signs people carried read, "COVID + Prison = Death," "Halt solitary," "Black Lives Matter," and "People not Cages." The protest was met with little movement by the state. As the families of prisoners noted in their protests and media engagements, in the context where no prisoners were being released due to COVID, the largest volume of movement inside and outside the prison came from the guards, who were able to return home to their families.

With over five hundred positive cases in a city of less than thirty thousand people, the ECF outbreak made Elmira into a hotspot. In Governor Andrew Cuomo's zoned plan of targeted school and business closures, that meant children in Elmira were returned to online schooling and bars and restaurants were takeout only. It was clear to anyone in the area: the City of Elmira was on lockdown because of the high number of cases in the prison, with the city and the ECF imagined as two contiguous spaces tightly sealed off from one another. Due to COVID cases in the prison, the notion that the prison was a part of the city was on the mind of Elmirans more than at any other time I can recall. After nearly two decades of following the politics of the prison in Elmira, I can't think of any other time when the health and well-being of prisoners was thought of as directly related to health and well-being of Elmirans on the outside of the prison.

New York's politicians were still eager to put the state's COVID failures behind the veil of secrecy. Yet, the walls of the prison are porous, and the attempt to control these leaks of humanity from behind the walls is part of the carceral state's refusal to accept the prisoners as part of Elmira as a place.

Guarding the Home

The commissioner of the New York State DOCS offered some words of advice to the graduating class of the Correction Officers Training Academy in 2008: "Treat everyone as you would want him or her to treat you, including the inmates . . . Listen before you act or react . . . Make sure you laugh at least once a day at all of the crazy and silly situations you will find yourselves in . . . Do not take home your personal prison problems, and do not bring to work your personal home problems."[12] Correction officers' own narratives and the high rates of domestic violence and substance abuse among this cohort indicate that this separation is difficult to maintain. In particular, there is a significant body of literature about the high rate of domestic violence among police and prison

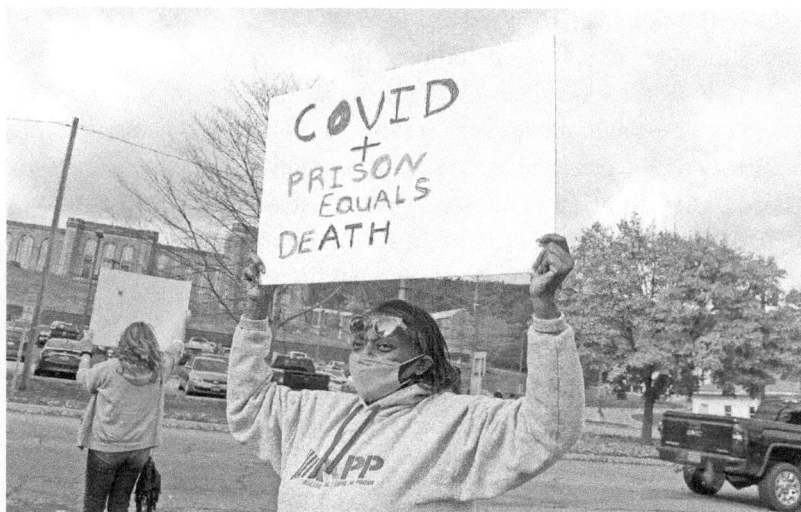

FIG. 8. "COVID = Death." Donna Robinson, a Buffalo resident and member of Release Aging People in Prisons, protests COVID policies outside of the Elmira Correctional Facility, October 27, 2020. Kate Collins—USA TODAY NETWORK, Binghamton Press & Sun-Bulletin via Imagn Content Services, LLC.

guards, research produced in parallel to the massive expansion of the criminal justice system in the 1970s, '80s, and '90s. Indeed, literature on domestic violence generally has shown a strong correlation between the cultures of policing and what Johnson, Todd, and Subramian called "authoritarian spillover" into the home: "Given that police officers receive both explicit/implicit societal approval for being in control and specific occupational training for exerting force when faced with uncontrollable situations, this spillover was to be expected."[13] Similar patterns have been found for those in the military, where workers "bring home" their work.[14] The "skills" of prison work come into conflict with other realms of correctional officers' lives—as fathers, husbands, friends, and coaches. The violence of prison guards in their homes demonstrates the fiction of a clean boundary between home and prison. Understanding these connections is key to undoing the "common sense" of the prison and to seeing it as a place with necessarily porous boundaries.

One of the primary jobs of a prison guard is to supervise prisoners as they are moved from one part of the prison to the other—from mess hall back to the cell, from the yard to a work site, and on rare occasions, to places outside the prison, including funerals, "deathbed visits" to family, and hospital stays. This job requires exerting control over another person's freedom of movement. How does practicing this task in one's daily rounds at work change a person when they are at home? For many guards, the use of force necessary to escort an incarcerated man in shackles to his mother's funeral in another part of the state does not translate well to managing one's own children on a trip in the car. As the commissioner's aspirational statement demonstrates, a deep separation is required by correction officers between their workplace and their home lives to maintain the efficient operation of New York State's prisons and perhaps even to separate oneself mentally because of the constantly encountered brutality.

In my research, male prison guards' narratives of their relationships with women demonstrate how they enacted the "skills" and hierarchies gleaned from prison work. Michael Morgan did his best to shield his family from stories about his work in the prison, which he viewed as too violent or too sordid for women and children and misunderstood by civilians.

> The worst thing my wife knew one time was that one time I was involved in a riot and I was bloody after I was done. Not from me. But my shirt was covered in blood . . . Well, I go home that night and my shirt was a bloody mess. I walk in the house, my wife happened to be up. She says, "What's goin' on?" I says, "I'm fine. Nothing major." And I burned my shirt. And I threw off my shirt and threw it in the garbage. The wood stove actually. My wife and my family never knew some of the altercations I was in, nothing. 'Til now. I always felt that I was able to keep that life where it belonged. And my life out here where it belonged.

Whether or not some of his motivation for burning his bloody shirt came from a desire to destroy the evidence of a crime against an incarcerated man, destroying the shirt before entering the house provides a measure of distance between the repressive realm of the prison and his life with his family. Officer Conover, mentioned in chapter 4, writes about putting on his gear— "baton, latex glove holder, key clips," elements of the uniform—as a part of packaging up the emotions of his home life and preparing himself to enter the prison.[15]

One woman, who I met randomly before an interview and whose son had recently taken the test for prison guard, told me that a prison guard had to have a wife to help him calm down after work. She mimed looking over her shoulder as she said it, imitating an often-heard remark that correction officers have a difficult time not being "on guard" even when they are in their own homes. Like many law enforcement agents, cos described a difficulty letting go of their skills in social spaces outside of the prison.[16] A former prison guard remembered being in the prison as a place of conflict, recalling, "You get a crowd of people . . . you know how many years—actual years—I spent in mess halls? And hundreds of inmates that were thinking of fighting? You do it. It's all second nature." One's role, one's work as a jailer is seen as a set of learned skills that are difficult to limit outside of the jail.

A local domestic violence counselor was hesitant to say that correction officers were overrepresented among her clients in a batterers' support group. Rather, she noted that law enforcement officers more generally have "issues" with power and control. Carmen Vasquez, a retired civilian worker at the Greene Correctional Facility, related the experience of prison work to a battle: "It's just like sending them to a war because you have to be on guard all the time." The enemy, however real or imagined, is within striking distance. Jackie Zuretsky was married to a correction officer for eight years; she recounted to me how her husband used his "job skills" on her at home: "He knew how to beat me without leaving marks because they learn how to beat the inmates without leaving marks." She noted how his efforts to control her mimicked his work in the prison in eerie ways, including locking her out of the house and hiding her money, both mechanisms of control used by guards against incarcerated men. In her experience, correction officers certainly treated their wives like they treated the inmates; he would often beat her while still wearing his uniform.

Michael Morgan described to me very clearly how his relationship with his son was affected by his work as a guard. It was difficult for him to step away from physically dominating his son during an argument: "My one boy pushed my buttons once really hard after I was outta being a guard. And I snapped for just a second. And he was on a motorcycle, and he was off the motorcycle and he was on the ground and I was on top of him and I was gonna smack him. My wife went spaz. And I snapped to real quick and I felt really bad. I did, you feel real bad. He had it comin', though. He did have it comin'." Here, his use of the word "snapped" indicates that he crossed the border in and out of the more violent world of the prison. Michael's narrative of his encounter with his son reveals another theme in the gendered world created when correction officers come home: it is often women who are most conscious of how the prison affects the men in their lives. A few retirees noted that their wives or daughters were eager for their retirement and said that the retired men had changed and become more relaxed since their retirement.

Circulations in the Carceral City

In addition to meeting the intellectual and sometimes sexual needs of prisoners, bringing ethnic foods unavailable in prison, and maintaining social ties, visitors of incarcerated men and women are part of a system of care for prisoners in Elmira. This system is achieved not only through intimacy but also through millions of what I call "caretaking dollars" deposited into commissary accounts. For example, the purchase of $16,238.88 worth of shoes through the commissary by prisoners at the Elmira Correctional Facility (not to mention millions of dollars of office supplies and food items also from the commissary and food from the vending machines during visits) comes from money provided by family and friends "on the outside," as prisoners do not otherwise have access to money during their incarceration. A vast difference in the total cost of supplies provided to the Elmira and Southport Correctional Facilities points to a divergence in the visiting patterns at these institutions, and the even greater social isolation of men incarcerated at Southport when compared with the ECF. Officially, prisoners at the Southport Correctional Facility were often being held at the facility as retaliation for behaviors or actions at other prisons, but at the time of my research there was also an extraordinarily high number of men with mental health diagnoses in all solitary confinement facilities across the state.[17] At Southport, the lesser amount of money spent in commissaries, more infrequent visits, and poor mental health of the prisoners reflect a higher degree of isolation.

Southport as an all-solitary facility must also be understood in the context of three converging social crises: the gradual process of deinstitutionalization of psychiatric beginning in the 1950's, a national shortage of housing, and the rising criminalization of poverty. It is commonly noted that many of the severely mentally ill who were not properly served by community mental clinics ended up in jail or prison. Simultaneously, Ben-Moshe has argued that incarceration disables; that being in solitary confinement causes people to become mentally unwell.[18] These men, referred to by staff as "bugs," who scream all night and bang their heads against the walls, are often the men who are deemed the most "troublesome" to be controlled and are thus moved to Special Housing Units. Jack Johnson, a local defense lawyer who represents many prisoners in Chemung County criminal court cases, suggested that 50 percent of prisoners at the facility are seriously mentally ill. So few men get visitors at Southport that there is a lesser need for a visitors' program. These men appear to be even more socially isolated from their families than prisoners at a maximum-security facility. I attribute this set of characteristics overall to the very different relationship Southport has to Elmira City when compared with the ECF.

Criminal Courts in the Carceral City

One of the most under-discussed aspects of the social life of a prison town is the fact that all the crimes that occur in the state prison facilities are tried in the Chemung County court system by Elmira judges with local attorneys as representatives for the county and the inmate. This includes guard-on-inmate crime, inmate-on-inmate crime, and crimes involving prisoners or their visitors engaged in contraband. One district attorney estimates that 30 percent of the felonies tried in Chemung County's courts are prosecution of crimes that occur within the prisons. According to one local public defender, an "extraordinary amount of our time is spent defending crimes that occur within prison."

Despite some people being ineligible to serve on juries because they work for the prisons or are related to law enforcement officers, Jack Johnson says that he finds that the juries are quite fair and that there is a 50 percent acquittal rate on the cases. He adds that "the inmates are scared to death—'We're gonna have an all-white jury, and I'm a Black guy, we're in town, I'm an inmate'—But our juries are fair." Johnson concludes that most juries are skeptical of prison guards, even in a town where prison work can be well regarded. "The thing that's interesting about defending inmates . . . and I don't think people realize it, if you look at our popular culture, every movie, TV show, and anything that's ever set in a prison setting, the inmate is the good guy and the guard is the bad guy, and that is in the back of people's heads. So that if you can paint a good picture about how hard this guy's life is in prison and that these guys make it worse, you can give them a plausible story, well, most of the time, that version wins out."

When I asked him to elaborate, he added, "Our acquittal rate is way better than it is anywhere else. So, I can't conclude that the juries are bigoted because they are more often than not ruling for the [prisoner] over the state. I don't think so. I mean. I'm sure that there are bigots out there, and God knows during jury selection we get a bunch of hands going up [when asked whether they have family who work for DOCS]. Part of the hardest part of my job is trying to convince these guys that you know you are probably going to get a fair trial and it is in your interest rather than copping a deal if you think you've got the chance." Johnson's analysis of the racial politics of inmate trials in Chemung County courts may indicate that while the law-and-order element remains firmly entrenched, there remains tension in some the city residents' relationship to the prisons, or it may not. If he is right, this divergence suggests a separation between common-sense notions of justice and the enactment of justice when presented with a real interaction between jailers and inmate from the prison. The circuit of interactions between social services, law enforcement and courts, and between prisoners and residents of the prison town suggests a need to theorize the prison town as a place of circulation of people and of resources.

Thinking of the prison as a porous place, as a place that leaks out into the prison town through the courts, through human relationships, through money and through our bodies requires that we think of prison not as a place that moves *freely* but simply as a place that moves.

6   Prison Visiting in a Prison Town

At the foot of the Elmira Correctional Facility, looked down upon by the main brick building on the "Hill," sits a small prefabricated building with yellow siding that houses the prison's visitors' center. The building is set apart from the prison by a large, tiered parking lot and hundreds of steps up to the front entrance of the facility. On weekends, the front entrance ramp of the hospitality center is busy with people talking, planning, preening their children, smoking, or waiting to be called for their visit to an incarcerated man. In the late 1990s, when the building first opened, there were some complaints from neighbors that the architecture of the building didn't match the more ornate nineteenth-century style of the prison or the neatly kept houses of the working-class residential neighborhood surrounding it. Others complained that the construction of the building was unnecessary—that it was more needless indulgence of inmates and their families. Today, however, the building has become integrated into the built environment of the city. Julia, a five-year volunteer at the facility, said of the prison, "It is a formidable institution. From the road it looks like a fortress." Other than the correction officers, and the movements of prisoners within and across the system, the visitors to the ECF are the only regular conduit of exchange into and out of the prison town.

Contrasted with the intimidating brick building surrounded by a double perimeter fence with razor wire atop the outermost fence, the pale-yellow aluminum siding of the hospitality center is more welcoming. Inside the center there is a large desk at the front of the room where volunteers check people in and help to prepare visitors' paperwork. It is a simple, almost industrial space: there is a bathroom, an area for children's toys, a few decorations on the walls, and folding tables and chairs.

Cheerful curtains in a country print, sewn by a volunteer, decorate the windows. Every Saturday and Sunday, the visitors' center building is the first stop for every visitor to the ECF. When entering, women, men and children stop and check in with the coordinator who helps them organize the paperwork necessary for them to visit—birth certificates for the children and state-issued identification for the adults. Each visitor is eager to have the first visit of the day, as the longer a visitor waits, the more likely that their visit will be canceled, or "terminated" in DOCS jargon, as there is often not enough time allotted to get all visitors into the prison in a single day. Visitors use the restroom, change their clothes and fix their hair, have a cup of tea, or just stretch their legs while they wait. If it is a long wait, visitors from further distances are given preference over "local" visitors, who can more easily return (in the mind of DOCS) during a less busy time.

When people are called to visit, they walk up the hundreds of stairs to the front door of the prison. "They will get you," says one visitor about the massive steps to the ECF. "They will get you even if you're really well and healthy." On the weekends, a volunteer drives elderly and disabled visitors to the top of the step. Perhaps unsurprisingly, for many Elmirans, including correction officers, the treatment of the families of incarcerated men becomes synonymous with the treatment of the criminality and "badness" of the prisoners. Volunteers at the visitors center often describe themselves as a buffer between the families of incarcerated men and the correction officers—a complicated and often heated set of relationships. For visitors to the ECF who arrive early in the morning on overnight buses from New York City or drive from across the state, Elmira the city is encapsulated by their experiences with correction officers and stops at fast food restaurants along the way. But no matter where they come from, visitors are often scared of their potential or historical maltreatment at the hands of the guards.

In the late 1990s, a member of a Christian social justice group that met at Mount Savior Monastery, the home of a Catholic order of brothers located in the rural hills of Chemung County outside Elmira, was troubled by the sight of young mothers standing in the rain with their children while waiting for a visit with their loved one. She brought her concern to the group, and together they sought a way to provide services and shelter based on their Christian belief in what they call "ministry." After research, they found that every weekend three thousand people visited Upstate prisons on buses from New York City alone, and that visits were considered essential by many DOCS administrators and scholars to keeping the prisoners in touch with their families, an important part of maintaining connections with home while people are incarcerated. Group members went to the prison parking lot on Saturday mornings, got on the buses and spoke with visitors to figure out their needs. Eventually, they called their project the "Dorothy Day Center," after the founder of the Catholic worker movement who started communal houses and farms for the poor and preached a radical doctrine of distributism. They later changed the name to the Elmira Visitor's Center to reflect and recruit a more ecumenical group of volunteers. After four years of meetings, DOCS gave volunteers a space inside the prison for the area's first welcome center for the families of the men incarcerated at Elmira, one of dozens of similar hospitality centers in the state. A few years later, the Department of Correctional Services built the yellow building at the foot of the prison to house the hospitality center.

In November 2006 the visitors' center was open nine days. On those nine days, there were 1018 visitors, 168 of whom were men, 628 women, and 222 children. One hundred and two, or slightly less than 10 percent, were categorized as local. A plurality of the visits were by people from New York City (277), with other concentrations of individuals from across New York State's metropolitan areas: Buffalo (98), Syracuse (128), and Rochester (224). Despite the distance and walls between them, each of these visitors represents an extraordinary amount of care work done for men in the prison by their families and lovers. Lillian Tillson, a Black Brooklynite who has visited two husbands and a brother in the ECF and other Upstate prisons over the last forty years, described the long bus ride from New York City to these institutions: "The bus. Sometimes you don't sleep. Maybe you can't get to sleep. So, you stay up [until 1 a.m.] to meet the bus. You fry you some food . . . [w]alking into a prison, being checked, like I had no substance, but like I was a second-class citizen because I was coming to see someone locked up." She said that there was such a huge build up for a visit—"I'm going on June twenty-fifth!"—so that there was tremendous disappointment if something prevented it.

Lillian outlines both the chaos created in her life by having a loved one incarcerated across the state and the level of control this creates over one's social life. Although she first visited her husband and then her brother in New York's prisons, Lillian empathized with women who left their sons behind in the jail after the visit: "A mother is realizing that she is leaving her son with these people. Will they protect him?"

There are a series of what are called "gate-side" visitors' hospitality centers at least partially funded by the Patmos Foundation based in New York City. f Indeed, although many people erroneously believe that the center is funded with public monies, following state law the majority of funding comes from volunteer hours and fundraisers. Volunteers raise money from private donations and fundraising projects like the sale of flowers. During my fieldwork, there were also donations from "inmate organizations," like the ECF branch of the NAACP, which donated cookies for families visiting on Christmas Day. Despite initial concerns by the funders that they don't actually help "local people," the hospitality center has received small grants from the Community Foundation of Elmira, a grant maker for small nonprofits in Elmira. In addition, the center receives $15,000 dollars a year from the Department of Correctional Services that apparently comes from a fund created thanks to the ridiculous cost of phone usage by prisoners. Visitors also give donations from time to time. Yvette noted that when she visited her husband at Wende Correctional Facility near Buffalo, there was a civilian taking "voluntary" donations for the center who made it abundantly clear that the donations were not considered voluntary.

Yvette now visits her husband every few months at Clinton Correctional Facility in the north country near the Canadian border. She takes the bus to the prison town and pays sixty-five dollars a night for a hotel room. If she stays for a forty-six-hour trailer visit, there is an extra sixty dollar charge for the hotel owner to drive Yvette and all of her things to the prison for the visit. Yvette brings money to purchase food to prepare meals during their trailer visit and to add to her husband's commissary account. To this must be added the cost of calling her husband a few times a week during times between visits. He can't be one of these "spoiled men," Yvette added, expecting a call every day. (However, she participated in the organized call-out against the exorbitant cost of the phone service in the spring of 2006.) She cringes at the way she is spending her money to maintain her relationship with her husband. Working as she does in childcare and other low-wage jobs, these expenses are a huge portion of her income. "Like the woman in the hotel where I stay, Leonore, she tells me that she gets the guards that come there and they, you know, they live there for about a week, and tell her all the horror stories. It's just unbelievable," she says. "And she tells me that her hotel is running because of the prison. I mean, that's not very nice to hear, you know, my money that I could be spending taking care of myself is going to a prison-run hotel, basically. That's what I call them." Of the myriad businesses that spring up to cater to the families of prisons, or existing businesses that expand on account of the income from families of prisoners, hotels are often the biggest beneficiaries.

On top of physically and financially taxing travel, Maria Adamzisk described the experience of going through the security clearance as the worst part of the visit. She recalled the "humiliation" of having to take off her bra when going through the metal detector. DOCS warns women to wear non-underwire bras, for fear that the wires could be turned into a weapon, but Maria said, "I don't have these 32As that these young women have, and if your bra has more than two hooks, you're gonna get beeped," that is, required to remove your bra in the bathroom before you enter the prison. Despite the humbling experience of visiting, Maria drives more than two hundred miles to visit her husband a few times a month, including trailer visits. When I interviewed Maria in her home, she showed me a bag of prepared foods in a back bedroom that she buys as she sees sales and saves for her husband. Her husband's next package included noodle soups, crackers, and canned meat that are deemed acceptable by DOCS policy. The collective work of Lillian, Yvette, and Maria is a part of the social reproduction of urban life in New York.

"Have a Cup of Tea"

The work of the visitor's center is decidedly mundane—getting coffee, helping with paperwork, providing snacks and coloring books for the children. Yet, according to volunteers, including a few women who frequently visit their husbands in other prisons, families of men incarcerated at Elmira are happy with the service. They are glad to have somewhere to sit and have a snack and clean up for their visit. Volunteers report that visitors are most happy that there is someone to watch their cell phones, which they are prohibited from bringing into the prison. DOCS rules for visiting include a dress code for visitors; volunteers are also charged with helping women who are deemed to be dressed too scantily to find additional clothes to cover themselves before entering the building. Hospitality center volunteers were proud of the quality of the services they provided, which they contrasted with the work of other centers across the state. Judy, a longtime volunteer, recalled that while visiting other hospitality centers, they found the one at the Attica Correctional Facility depressing and poorly cared for. This indicated to them the less welcoming environment of Attica the city more generally. According to Judy, for example, when clergy are hired at Attica churches, they must sign a contract stating that they will not do ministry in the prisons. Most of the tasks of the volunteers comprise basic communication between visitors and guards—asking maintenance to fix the toilets, negotiating where the smokers stand, and dealing with the hostility from rank-and-file correction officers. But in the minds of the volunteers, unlike Attica, the Elmira center is a symbol of welcoming the families of prisoners.

The volunteers at the center represented a counternarrative to the dominant role Elmirans play in the prison: guard and keeper. As is true for many volunteer-run organizations, the set of volunteers changes regularly. During my fieldwork, the center was run by a group of about sixteen volunteers, among them twelve white men and women, three African American women, and one Asian American woman. Noting that many of the women and men coming on the buses from New York City were African American, Priscilla Moore, an African American woman in her sixties, a longtime volunteer and a retired social worker, said of her decision to volunteer, "And, of course, being an African American, I knew I needed to do this. They [the visitors] needed to see a Black person greet them, to know that there are Black people in the community that want to help." In contrast to the many Elmirans, overwhelmingly white, who feared the families of incarcerated men as interlopers in their city, Priscilla sought to acknowledge the commonalities in the experience of African Americans and build a bridge with the visitors. She added that just greeting people who come to the center and saying "I know you're tired. Have a cup of tea" helped people to prepare for their visit. Jenny Mulvaney, a white working-class grandmother who is a frequent volunteer, recalled that her own brush with the law—a decades-old felony conviction—was on her mind the day hospitality center volunteers came to her church. Jenny was drawn to volunteer because "that could have been my family [coming to visit her in prison]." Jenny was only given probation but believed that others should have the same opportunity for redemption that she had. While Jenny identified with the struggles of the prisoners and those who visit them, she recounted to me that COS often told her that she would make a good CO. Her calm demeanor and her ability to talk to prisoners were good assets for both roles. She, too, had considered taking the civil service test for CO because she enjoyed working with the inmates (who worked alongside her as porters when the visitor center was still inside the prison) but declared that she was "too old to start something new."

Most of the volunteers and center board members were either a part of the original group of founders or were recruited from their churches. A sense of moral or religious mission often undergirds their decision to volunteer with the center. A few volunteers carefully noted that this was not a project of evangelism, but rather in the words of Irene, a local community college professor and longtime volunteer, "the motivation for most people getting involved is because of their faith, and we try to reach out to them [the visitors] in a loving way." Irene spoke about her work at the hospitality center in terms of a larger social project of caretaking: "And here they are, and they're gonna spend a day in this terrible place [the prison] in the visiting room and then get kicked out at 3:00 and get on a bus and go back to New York. What an incredible effort on their behalf—on behalf of this guy who's in prison. Then, I look at the numbers. On a busy day, we have one hundred visits. Well, the population at Elmira is eighteen hundred. Something like that. It's tiny. What about all of the rest of these guys? There's nobody."

This common strain of humanitarianism wove through the volunteers' work. Other volunteers expressed admiration for the men and women who come visit the prisoners. Heather, an African American social worker in her early forties, said, "They may be the nicest people in the world. But look at what they've just gone through. Getting their babies up out of the bed at one o'clock in the morning to go see whoever they are visiting in the prison. Which is beautiful. I couldn't do it. If it were my man, I'm not sure I could do it." Many volunteers noted the totality of the destructiveness of the prison, which they saw as injurious to both "keeper and captive." Volunteers clearly have a commitment to the men incarcerated at Elmira as persons who have experienced discrimination or limitations in their life experiences, or both, and included poems by prisoners about their incarceration in their first newsletter. True, not all of the volunteers did the work at the hospitality center with a sense of religious or moral mission: one young woman said she felt no particular affinity for prisons or prisoners. Rather, she shared that she felt a broader concern for social justice had started volunteering because she was "incredibly bored out of my mind" in Elmira and liked the work.

In recent years, the center has struggled to recruit new volunteers, as many aging members of the founding group have become less involved. I accompanied two senior citizen hospitality center volunteers, Stan and Allie, on an appointment at an Elmira city senior center in search of new volunteers. The first question asked of us, after we were introduced ourselves, was, "Are you all guards?" The woman gingerly explained that her daughter worked on "the Hill" and thought perhaps we might know her. Stan, a longtime center volunteer, explained that we were not guards but representatives of the visitors' center, looking for volunteers who could work with the families of inmates. Stan and Allie tried to garner support for the project by telling their audience of potential volunteers that the families of inmates, particularly children, are also victims of crime—the crimes of their loved ones having cost them a father. Most of the elderly members of the crowd had come for the free lunch, but there was a fundamental tension at work here: How does one present the work of hospitality to families of incarcerated men to a city where prisons are a dominant industry?

Earlier, Stan, who had worked and volunteered with prisoners for over thirty years, had shared, "I think the hospitality center is a good program. I think it really provides a needed service and provides a real connection point between the community and the prison in some way. It's kind of a less threatening connection, for a lot of people, than actually working with the prisoners, which is good." As Stan suggested, the prison is a place of apprehension, if not fear, for many local residents, and thus many are reluctant to engage the prison, particularly in a way that might be considered "pro-prisoner." While historically there have been more supportive interactions between at least one historically African American church congregation and the prison, the visitors' center is the only organization in the city of Elmira that works to bridge the gap—in many ways, to recognize the fact that while prisons are sources of jobs, they hold within them men who have families.

Guarding the Carceral City

Shedding light on the prison and the prisoners in a prison town reveals the tensions within the city about its role in the carceral state. As I discussed in chapter 4, families of prisoners are decidedly not welcome; their distorted ghosts haunt the racial politics of everyday policing in Elmira. Because of these tensions, the center tries to keep what one volunteer called a "low profile" over concern that attention might bring controversy and disrupt their work. There is an annual volunteer reception dinner, announcement of their activities in the local paper and church bulletins, and periodic open houses attended by the mayor. But for the most part, the center's functioning requires maintaining a balance between their favorable view by a relatively small group of Elmirans, the DOCS top level brass, and visitors, and the perceptions of some in Elmira who are hostile to incarcerated men and their needs. As Irene, the college professor, saw it, the act of welcoming was at the heart of the project of the hospitality center. In a half-hour news interview in 1997 when the center opened, she explained, "It has really been a privilege to get to know some of the people who spend all of their savings coming almost every week to come and visit their men . . . We want them to know that here in Elmira we admire their courage and there is a welcome for them."[1]

Correction officers' distrust of and distaste for prisoners and their families is not always so subtle. The volunteers are sometimes sneered at by guards who see them as "coddling the inmates." This hostility emerges in other ways, too. On one occasion when the visitor's center building was used by guards for a meeting, volunteers returned to find that the coffee urn had been ruined after it had been used as a spittoon for chewing tobacco, and "fuck these people" had been written on one of the tables. In the words of one correction officer, Greg Shaunessy, who during most of our interview had struck me as a rather mild man (in that he described never worrying about seeing inmates on the streets outside because he had treated them respectfully enough, which I began to take as a sign that men were less likely to be violent on the job), "Ninety percent of the time, the families are bigger scumbags than the inmates." There is, however, a generally tepid relationship between DOCS and the volunteers who run the center, with moments of tension. While volunteers often rolled their eyes at DOCS's bureaucratic requirements, members had to encourage a DOCS representative to sit at the table with the rest of the group during board meetings. One long-time volunteer called DOCS a "secretive agency" that allowed for little public scrutiny. He noted that volunteers had no idea what happened once the visitors went through the front door of the prison. The hospitality center was a friendly place to be, but once visitors entered the prison they were treated like "scumbags," just as the prisoners were. Nevertheless, volunteers felt their time was worth the effort.

There is a single correction officer who staffs the hospitality center along with two volunteers every weekend day. While many officers avoid the visitors' center when they can, there are still moments of hostility from the rank-and-file correction officers toward the volunteers. Stan spoke about a time he saw an officer he knew from the visiting area at a restaurant in town. The officer refused to acknowledge him and say hello, despite Stan's belief that the CO recognized him. There are also somewhat kinder moments; there is a suggestion box that sits on the table, mostly filled with notes from visitors thanking them for their work. One guard puts in a note every week suggesting that the coordinator be given a raise. Jenny commented on her relationship with the guards:

> In the beginning, I was interfering, but by the end of the day, they [the guards] appreciated it, they understood the service I was providing to make their jobs easier. There's officers who have their opinions about the visitors' center, and it's not a good opinion. They think we're just a bunch of bleeding-heart liberals and we're just there because we feel sorry for the inmates and they don't appreciate what we're

doing. They weren't real receptive to us when we opened up. They didn't want us there. It was the state who said we could do it . . . The officers who work with us, they get it. They say to me, "I could have used you this week on Thursday, I was swamped."

Considering prison visiting is one of the sole sites of contact between prisoners and their outside lives, it is not shocking that it is a site of surveillance and tension. It is these everyday experiences that shed light on the debates about how and what people and capital should circulate in a prison town.

On Not Visiting Southport

After what the Department of Correctional Services saw as the positive work of the visitors' center at the ECF, DOCS asked if they would also consider opening and staffing a hospitality center at the Southport Correctional Facility. Despite their concerns that they were already having some challenges staffing the current center, a group of volunteers toured the prison to consider the project. Virginia Armstrong, a visitors' center volunteer who participated in the tour, said of Southport that the visiting experience is vastly different there because it is an entirely Special Housing Unit prison. "It's like the old prison movies—there's the bar and you can put your hand through," and visitors are not allowed to hug. In addition, the numbers of visitors to Southport are significantly fewer than at the ECF. Other than the prisoners who work as porters helping to clean the prison, the men who are in solitary confinement get very few visits. Part of this pattern may be related to the fact that a move to Southport means being moved away from another facility for a generally short time as a punishment for behaviors in a regular maximum-security prison, often six months. However, there seems to be some suggestion that because there are very high numbers of men incarcerated in SHUs who have serious mental health problems, they are more estranged from their families; the lower number of visits may be indicative of an even greater level of social isolation than men at maximum security prisons typically experience. Lillian Tillman described visiting Southport as a qualitatively different experience than a "regular" maximum security prison:

The SHU, I didn't know what this was about. Oh, my brother looked so fearful in that place, he was shaking. They bring them to the room. Chains on their feet, chains on their hands. And you got the glass here, then you got this little grate, and then they can put their hands to touch you. But you I didn't really know the significance [of him being in a Special Housing Unit]. I heard he went to the SHU. But hell I didn't even know what the SHU was. You know, I used to watch those shows "Lockdown Raw." I didn't equate them as the same thing. I know he was locked in twenty-three hours. I just didn't put two and two together. You know, what I seen on TV seemed so foreign. Yeah, but he was there.

Largely due to their inability to provide volunteers at two facilities, board members of the visitor's center declined to open a center at Southport.

As I have shown in this chapter, people (those who come voluntarily and those who are forcibly compelled to come by the state) and capital (in amounts negligible to the state and meaningful for working-class families) circulate through the prison town. Salaries and the provision of a few commodities needed by prisoners are important sources of income provided by the prisons to the town despite the prison's drain on municipal resources. Prison visiting is also an important site of migration across the abandoned spaces of New York State. In prison visiting, the tensions of incarcerating thousands of men from across New York State emerge most clearly.

Conclusion

ABOLITION AND A FREE NEW YORK

In his collection of essays *History against Misery*, historian David Roediger writes that "almost never does the work of digging someone else's grave not involve excavating a part of our own," a point which he situates in miserabilism, in the surrealist tradition of Andre Bretón.[1] I have mulled over this sentence many times, but it returns to me most intractably when I view the image of a smiling white child, the granddaughter of then—Southport councilmember Samuel Criss, positioned next to a shovel at the groundbreaking for the Southport Correctional Facility in 1987. In this picture, a performance of growth and promise of job expansion in a time of deep decline across the working class, I see the decision to bury so many Black, Latino/a/x, and poor white New Yorkers in exchange for this poisonous morsel of hope. I see a willingness to choose deeply miserable work for the chance to go on a vacation, to send your children to Catholic school, to afford two cars, to enter the "middle class."

Rarely is this digging of graves a literal digging, but in the case of prison expansion as a jobs program for a struggling town, it was just that. Prisons and the carceral state do not produce social goods; a person's incarceration leaves a catastrophic wake of familial loss, of truncated lives, and of wasted breath. The collective experience of mass incarceration has wreaked havoc on Black and Latino/a/x communities and the racialized poor such that incarceration is often viewed as a rite of passage. It has severed the hands of organizations fighting for radical change inside and outside prison walls.[2] There is a parallel misery in prison work; prison jobs in Elmira have produced meager racialized advantages for prison guards and their families and simultaneously brought about an enduring and contradictory host of stigmas. The work itself is not valued, not prized, and, in the words of one guard who left after ten years at the Department of Corrections, his time as a prison guard "warped him." "I knew it was warping me because I started looking forward to it," he told me. "And it's not normal for somebody to look forward to going in and using force on a person, extreme force on a person to get him under control. And looking forward to it. Okay, it's not normal. It's not human nature. Or, it shouldn't be human nature, okay."

My commitment to the abolition of prisons and police came from a reckoning with the graveyards of my family and my hometown. This was a personal reckoning, of course—seeing photos of my grandfather teaching sheet metal to prisoners in a chapbook dedicated to the centennial anniversary of the Elmira Correctional Facility in the archives—but it was also about seeing my family and my town in the larger set of relationships of what I now understand as racial capitalism. As the granddaughter of two prison guards, I saw that my whitened family had been recruited to do the work of the carceral state in a place that had lost its shine and its value in global capitalism, a place that proved useful for the state as a prison town. This book, then, is not only an argument about the failure of prisons as an economic development project and a jobs program, which is certainly true, but also an argument that we should view the prison as a part of a system that creates misery at all scales of human life. In order to unmake the miserable conditions of Elmira inside the prisons and out, we have to shut down the prisons and to build a society that is built on human solidarity. As abolitionists Berger, Kaba, and Stein have argued, "The stubborn immediacy of the demand [for abolition] disturbs those who hope for resolution of intractable social problems within the confines of the existing order."[3] Abolition is an essential goalpost, lest we settle for access to a few hundred "shitty" jobs incarcerating our Black, Brown, and poor neighbors.

In this book, I have tried to frame this scene of white complicity—a relatively powerful man's grandchild with a white bonnet and a shovel—within the context of the history of New York and its political economy. When I first started this project as a graduate student, I met a movement leader from Newark, New Jersey, as a part of a campaign of poor people's organizations. I told her that I was studying prison towns and prison guards, and she looked at me squarely and said, "Make sure you write that it's bad for people on both sides of the prison walls." Her words have stuck with me over the years, as I struggle with this tension between prison guard and prisoner in my writing, teaching, and organizing. Abolitionism requires that the *relationships* created in systems of brutality be examined in dialectical form. It is not a facile answer to say that both jailer and jailed are harmed by the carceral state and the new formulations of race, class, and gender it created. We know that guards have higher rates of suicide, alcohol, and drug addiction, and death than other classes of workers and that they often view the job as a mechanism to have material and social access, not as a source of pride.[4] Prisons themselves are sources of social chaos, breaking human connections with a keen form of brutality. As prison numbers dwindle in New York State, undoing some of the chaos caused by prison expansion, as abolitionists we must keep an unflinching eye on the chaos that prison expansion in Elmira sought to keep at bay: unemployment and state disinvestment. What this project, and other projects focused on prison expansion show, is that the purpose of prison expansion is rooted in capitalist crisis; a true, human solution to the crisis must focus on alleviating desperation, hunger, and need. What does that human solution look like, and how do we fight for it? How do we build it?

How Do We Build Abolition?

Prisons are a force of racialization and impoverishment. Prison expansion and mass incarceration were not natural or inevitable; politicians and coalitions of the advantaged (however a person is or one images oneself as advantaged), wealthy, and powerful went to bat for this "solution" to the crises of the era. I have argued in *Prison Town* that prison guards emerge from doing the grunt work of the carceral state stained and broken by its brutalities. And, as many guards told me, no one wants their son to work in the prison. An abolitionist future is built on working lives that people can come home from, jobs that don't leave us always looking over our shoulder, shedding harshness into our living rooms. In whose interests is it for these conditions and the inequalities they protect to endure? It is useful to think about what could have been built *instead* of a new prison in 1988. What other infrastructures could the state have invested in that would have given Elmira, Brooklyn, Rochester, Buffalo, or Oswego, more of the good life that we all deserve and less misery? I believe the answer lies in this history: when Elmira's boosters testified to the benefits of the prison, they were not eager to advance the incarceration of others (although for some that was a welcome social policy), they were eager for jobs. If in 1985, an alternative plan to "help Upstate" were presented to Elmira from Albany, offering the same capital to build infrastructure and to pay four hundred to six hundred workers livable salaries to teach and work in schools and to expand public transit, to build alternative energy capacity and regional rail lines—where would the city be now? An improved public transit system would certainly help the rural area of the county, too, where without a car, you don't have access to much of anything. As small towns and rural areas continue to see the crumbling of their housing and health-care infrastructure and experience the barriers created by lack of access to broadband internet, the question of why prisons and what next is even more urgent. Local politicians have railed against big government spending for social programs for generations, while simultaneously pushing for huge capital expenditures for prison expansion. This history can provide us a road map for the future. If we imagine our future together, what could we and should we build?

Abolition is not simply about the subtraction of the infrastructure of control and punishment—although that is certainly crucial—but it is also about the building of a society that centers the needs of all people. Rather than giveaways to enrich the wealthy, we have an opportunity to share the abundance of our society and reimagine our relationships to work, to the land, to the places where we want to live and choose to stay. Access to the material needs of life—equally, across the demarcations of race, of language, of immigration status—is the materiality of abolition. Some have critiqued this form of abolitionism as a social movement guide as too idealistic, too romantic, and too impossible; I disagree. Abolitionism allows us to envision the infrastructures of the world we want. It is those radical demands that can guide movements for social change that can think beyond prettier prisons to forms of governance that make our world whole.

Notes

Introduction

1. All names have been changed to protect the anonymity of the people who took part in the research. In some instances, people appear as amalgamations of interlocutors to further obscure identifying information. The names of people holding public office or those who have been named in historical media have not been changed.
2. Throughout the book, I choose to use the terms "prisoner" or "incarcerated person," following the lead of formerly incarcerated people who note the dehumanization of prison language. Where I use the term inmate, I am following the lead of interlocutors who used the term in their descriptions of events.
3. Coughlin, "Report of Operations and Development"; Aiken, "Era of Mass Expansion."
4. Bureau of Justice Statistics, *Key Statistics, Total Correctional Population*.
5. Eason, *Big House on the Prairie*.
6. U.S. Census Bureau, "U.S. Census Bureau QuickFacts," 2010 and 2023.
7. Vera Institute of Justice, "Empire State of Incarceration."
8. Hooks et al., "Prison Industry," 37–57.
9. Eason, *Big House on the Prairie*, 5, 81.
10. Marx's original reads, "Men make their own history, but they do not make it as they please; they do not make it under self-selected circumstances, but under circumstances existing already, given and transmitted from the past." Marx, *Eighteenth Brumaire of Louis Bonaparte*. This was foundational in the teaching of Dr. Leith Mullings in how to understand the anthropological approach to political economy. Mullings, *On Our Own Terms*.
11. See Bill Roseberry's argument that such anthropologies, across a wide range of topics, "offer a fundamental challenge to those who discuss culture, history, and practice without sufficient consideration of class, capitalism, and power." In his 1988 article in the *Annual Review of Anthropology* on the history of political economy, Roseberry writes that scholars doing political

economy, seeking to understand "particular conjunctions" of global/local, determination/freedom, structure/agency, "must avoid making capitalism too determinative, and they must avoid romanticizing the cultural freedom of anthropological subjects." Roseberry, "Political Economy," 174. Roseberry's refusal to cleave structure from agency employs the analytical subtlety required to explain the workings of power in everyday life. "What requires stressing," he notes, "is the unity of structure and agency, the activity of human subjects in structured contexts that are themselves the products of past activity but, as structured products, exert determinative pressures and set limits upon future activity" Roseberry, "Political Economy," 172.

12. Roseberry, "Hegemony and the Language of Contention," 364.
13. Wacquant, "Deadly Symbiosis," 95–133; Goffman, *Asylums*.
14. Pisciotta, *Benevolent Repression*.
15. Benavides, "Elmira Reformatory," 1126–28.
16. Horigan, *Elmira*.
17. New York State Department of Corrections of Community Supervision, "DOCCS FACT SHEET."
18. T. Lueck, "Declining Elmira Buoyed by Plant Reopening," *New York Times*, June 2, 1985.
19. Smith and New York State, "In the Matter of a Public Hearing."
20. Harvey, "From Managerialism to Entrepreneurialism," 4.
21. Harvey, "From Managerialism to Entrepreneurialism."
22. Murakawa, *First Civil Right*.
23. City of Elmira, "City of Elmira, Budget Worksheet Proposed."
24. Paul Davidson, "Just Two Cities Are in Recession. Who's Unhappy? Elmira, New York and Danville, Illinois," *Hagertown Herald-Mail/Herald-Mail Media*, February 25, 2019, https://www.heraldmailmedia.com/story/news/2019/02/25/just-two-cities-are-in-recession-whos-unhappy-elmira-new-york-and-danville-illinois/44261315/.
25. Gilmore, "Extraction."
26. Harvey, *Condition of Postmodernity*, 125–26.
27. Gramsci, as quoted in Harvey, *Condition of Postmodernity*.
28. Muehlebach and Shoshan, "Introduction," 317.
29. Pappas, *Magic City*.
30. Gilmore, *Golden Gulag*.
31. Harvey, *Condition of Postmodernity*, 136.
32. Martin, "Historicizing White Nostalgia."
33. Smith and New York State, "In the Matter of a Public Hearing."
34. Harvey, *Condition of Postmodernity*; Kasmir, "Mondragón Model as Post-Fordist Discourse," 379–400.

35. New York State Department of Corrections and Community Supervision, "Quarterly Workforce Report."
36. New York State Department of Corrections and Community Supervision and Dworakowski, "Under Custody Report."
37. Wagner and Kopf, "Racial Geography of Mass Incarceration."
38. New York State Department of Correctional Services, "Quarterly Workforce Report." The Department of Corrections made this information available to me in 2008 but declined to give me updated information after that. Michael Schwirtz, Michael Winerip, and R. Gabeloff, "The Scourge of Racial Bias in New York State Prisons," *New York Times*, December 3, 2–16.
39. Robinson, *Black Marxism*.
40. Burton makes the argument that the expansion of prisons in New York State in the 1980s was also led by DOCS desire to geographically divide and disperse incarcerated Black radical organizers. Burton, *Tip of the Spear*; Berger, *Captive Nation*.
41. Du Bois, *Black Reconstruction in America*.
42. Seigel, *Violence Work*, 76–85.
43. When this story of prison expansion is told in California, or even in counties closer to New York City, it is Black and Brown New Yorkers who are recruited to do the work of policing. New York City's police force—despite the endurance of its decidedly white and Irish-American leadership—is now only one-third white. Greg Smith, "Number of Black Patrol Cops Falls as NYPD Upper Ranks Remain Majority White," *City*, June 24, 2020.
44. For a history of the rebellion at Auburn prison that was a precursor to the Attica Rebellion, see Burton, "Minimum Demands," 13–16 and Burton, *Tip of the Spear*.
45. Casanova, *Each One Teach One*.
46. Narayan, "How Native Is a 'Native' Anthropologist?" 671.

1. Deindustrialization

1. "Jamaicans, at Foundry, Took Jobs to See What U.S. Is Like," *Star-Gazette*, September 26, 1944; "15 Jamaicans Join Chemung Foundry Staff," *Star-Gazette*, November 4, 1944.
2. "Foundry Asks Jamaicans Remain Here," *Star-Gazette*, April 15, 1946; "Foundry Gets Contract for Castings," *Star-Gazette*, March 14, 1945; "Union Ready for Strike at Foundry," *Star-Gazette*, January 14, 1946; "Warning Repeated on Employment of Jamaicans," *Star-Gazette*, May 15, 1945; "Jamaicans Express Sincere Thanks," *Star-Gazette*, July 2, 1946; "Income Tax Correction Rush Abates," *Star-Gazette*, March 29, 1945.

3. The regional racial hierarchies within the United States give rise to the patterns of mass incarceration, as prisons are always connected to the lives of working-class people. See Rhodes, *Total Confinement*; Waldram, "Anthropology in Prison"; Schept, *Coal, Cages, Crisis*.

4. Hahamovitch, *No Man's Land*, 15.

5. I came to the story of James and Eustace through the story of the carceral state, but the story of Jamaican workers recruited to do industrial work in New York State in 1944 adds to the collective story of the immigrant experience and the making of race in the United States in the postwar period. This is a slight corrective or additive to the dominant history of guestworkers during this period: while the Bracero Program was the largest and most significant program, the recruitment of guest workers by the U.S. government or, later, through U.S. companies, went beyond Mexico, and after 1942 included German Prisoners of War, the Bahamas, British Honduras (now Belize), Costa Rica, Barbados, and Newfoundland, Canada (Driscoll, *Tracks North*, 68; Hahamovitch, *No Man's Land*). While the dominant story told is that workers given temporary visas during this period were purely agricultural, in Elmira, Jamaican workers were doing industrial work and in the southern United States, Mexican workers were working on the railroads (Driscoll, *Tracks North*). Expanding the idea of who guestworkers were—and are—shifts the narrative of race-making in the US.

6. Gilmore, *Golden Gulag*, 15.

7. For an example of how new formations of racial capitalism following the crises of deindustrialization emerge through the health care system in Pittsburgh, see Winant, *Next Shift*.

8. Morrell, "'Municipal Welfare' and the Neoliberal Prison Town."

9. Muehlebach and Shoshan, "Introduction," 317.

10. Harvey, *Condition of Postmodernity*, 136.

11. Martin, "Historicizing White Nostalgia."

12. Huling, "Building a Prison Economy in Rural America."

13. U.S. Census Bureau, "Elmira City, Chemung County, New York," accessed October 3, 2024, https://data.census.gov/profile/Elmira_city,_Chemung_County,_New_York?g=060XX00US3601524229.

14. United States Tariff Commission, "Calculators, Typewriters, and Typewriter Parts."

15. "Obituary, M. K. Smykowski, Rand Retiree," *Star-Gazette*, 1995.

16. Andy Lamb, "Strange Keyboard Orders Filled Easily at Rem Rand," *Elmira Advertiser*, November 26, 1955.

17. "Rand Chief Says Layoffs Won't Top 860: New Products Planned Here," *Star-Gazette*, September 22, 1960.

18. James Hare, "Elmira History: A Boom Town in the 1940's," *Star-Gazette*, October 14, 2016.

19. A handful of obituaries noting previous employment at Remington Rand exist before 1990. I chose to focus on the years 1990–2000 because of the large number of obituaries during this period noting Remington Rand employment.

20. Roediger, *Working toward Whiteness*.

21. Omi and Winant, *Racial Formation in the United States*; Sugrue, *Origins of the Urban Crisis*.

22. U.S. Bureau of the Census, "1970 Census of Population: Characteristics of the Population, Volume 1, Part A, New York," accessed October 3, 2024, https://usa.ipums.org/usa/resources/voliii/pubdocs/1970/Population/Vol1/1970a_ny1-02.pdf; U.S. Census Bureau, "Decennial Census, DEC Demographic and Housing Characteristics, Table P8, 2020," accessed October 3, 2024, https://data.census.gov/table/DECENNIALDHC2020.P8?q=Elmira Black population.

23. George Osgood, "EFA Grad Made the Cut with All Who Knew Him," *Star-Gazette*, November 2, 1994.

24. Denise Clay, "Elmiran Was 'Ahead of Her Time'," *Star-Gazette*.

25. Sugrue, *Origins of the Urban Crisis*.

26. Facebook posts accessed February 2020. For a similar pattern in Easton, Pennsylvania, following urban renewal, see Smith and Eisenstein, *Rebuilding Shattered Worlds*.

27. Pappas, *Magic City*.

28. Manuel-Scott, "Soldiers of the Field."

29. Hahamovitch, *No Man's Land*, 59.

30. Hahamovitch, *No Man's Land*.

31. García-Colón, *Colonial Migrants at the Heart of Empire*; Flores, *Grounds for Dreaming*; Findlay, *We Are Left without a Father Here*; Molina, *How Race Is Made in America*.

32. Manuel-Scott noted the significant cost for poor Jamaicans to prepare themselves for the recruitment center, in addition to height, weight, and health requirements. Manuel-Scott, "Soldiers of the Field."

33. "Warning Repeated on Employment of Jamaicans," *Star-Gazette*, May 15, 1945.

34. Daniel Aloi, "Looking at WWII through Local Eyes," *Star-Gazette*, April 11, 1993.

35. "Jamaicans, at Foundry, Took Jobs to See What U.S. Is Like," *Star-Gazette*, September 26, 1944.

36. "Questions and Answers," *Star-Gazette*, December 31, 1945.

37. Dick Mitchell and Jeb Kresge, "Layoffs Not New to Rand Workers," *Star-Gazette*, January 23, 1972.

38. Kate Fleisher and Ansley Rambeau, "Caught in the Middle," *Star-Gazette*, January 23, 1972.

39. Fleisher and Rambeau, "Caught in the Middle."

40. Fleisher and Rambeau, "Caught in the Middle."

41. Carmen Christie, "Former Prison Officer 'Friendly and Outgoing,'" *Star-Gazette*, November 28, 1990.

42. Compiled from New York State Department of Labor, Labor Statistics and compared with U.S. Census 2000 maps.

43. During the period covered in this book, the title of the relevant department in New York State has changed from the Department of Correctional Services to the Department of Corrections and Community Supervision; for the sake of simplicity I have used the abbreviation DOCS throughout.

44. In the case of central Appalachia, prison expansion and tourism are not mutually exclusive. Judah Schept describes this process in depth in his book *Coal, Cages, Crisis*. He notes that in the case of turning the former Brushy Mountain Penitentiary in Tennessee into a prison themed distillery, the refuse of previous carceral infrastructure has been turned into a tourist site in which outlaw becomes an aesthetic.

2. Southport Correctional Facility

1. Smith and New York State, "In the Matter of a Public Hearing."

2. T. Lueck, "Declining Elmira Buoyed by Plan Reopening," *New York Times*, June 2, 1985.

3. Tese, "Rebuilding New York."

4. "Other Applicants for Zone Program," *New York Times*, January 19, 1987; Marc Uhligs, "New York Names First 10 Sites as Special Development Zones: State Lists 10 Development Zones," *New York Times*, July 2, 1987.

5. Harvey, *Condition of Postmodernity*.

6. For "transfer payments" see Mullings, "Losing Ground," 1–21. For the concept of a growth coalition bloc, see Logan and Molotch, *Urban Fortunes*. For more significant analysis of the Gramscian roots of term "bloc," see Woods, *Development Arrested*, 17.

7. Cronon, *Nature's Metropolis*, 19 and xiv.

8. Murakawa, *First Civil Right*; Berger, *Captive Nation*.

9. Murakawa, *First Civil Right*, 3.

10. Hinton, *From the War on Poverty to the War on Crime*.

11. Center for Behavioral Health Statistics and Quality, "National Survey on Drug Use and Health (NSDUH)."

12. Gilmore, "Beyond the Prison Industrial Complex." See also Burch, "Scripting the Conviction," 645–57.

13. Peter Kihss, "State Prisons, Filled Over Capacity Cut Back Sharply on Rikers Intake: Frantic Commissioner Trying to Lease Federal Space in His Search for Expedients to Admit Newcomers.," *New York Times,* June 28, 1981.

14. Peter Kihss, "New York Group Opposing Bond Issue for Prisons. New York Times," *New York Times,* June 28, 1981.

15. Kihss, "State Prisons, Filled Over Capacity Cut Back Sharply on Rikers Intake."

16. Clyde Haberman, "Carey and Koch Back Bond Issue on State Prisons," *New York Times,* October 10, 1981; Haberman, "Koch Terms the Apparent Defeat of Prison Bond Plan 'Outrageous,'" *New York Times,* November 10, 1981.

17. Haberman, "Carey and Koch Back Bond Issue"; Haberman, "Koch Terms the Apparent Defeat."

18. Frank Lynn, "13934 48% Yes, 52% No: Carey Cites Fund Limits On Expanding Prisons: Final Prison Bond Vote," *New York Times,* November 11, 1981.

19. John Kelleher, "Prison Bond Issue Debate Rolls On," *Star-Gazette,* October 12, 1981.

20. E. J. Dionne, "New York Expects to Expand Prisons despite Bond Vote: 2600 Beds by Mid-'82; but Correction Aide Cites Lack of Money for the Support of Additional Beds," *New York Times,* November 28, 1981; Josh Barbanel, "Cuomo to Seek Bonds of U.D.C. for Prison Cells: Move Would Avoid Need for Vote by the Public," *New York Times,* January 26, 1983.

21. "Judge Dismisses Suit on Prison Financing," *New York Times,* December 21, 1983.

22. Smith, *New Urban Frontier.*

23. Joseph Fried, "The Urban Development Corporation Changes Course and Survives," *New York Times,* July 15, 1979.

24. Phillips-Fein, *Fear City.*

25. Tese, "Rebuilding New York."

26. Tese, "Rebuilding New York."

27. Michael Oreskes, "State to Build 5 New Prisons, Including One in the Bronx," *New York Times,* June 25, 1983.

28. Oreskes, "State to Build 5 New Prisons."

29. Oreskes, "State to Build 5 New Prisons."

30. "Double Dose of Good News," *Star-Gazette,* February 26, 1986.

31. Proceedings of the County Legislature Chemung County, "Proceedings of the County Legislature Chemung County," 85–171 §.

32. Proceedings of the County Legislature Chemung County, "Proceedings of the County Legislature Chemung County," 85–171 §.

33. Jerry Gleeson, "Council Also Urges Cuomo to Approve Prison Site," *Star-Gazette,* 1985.

34. Gleeson, "Council Also Urges Cuomo to Approve Prison Site."

35. Southern Tier Economic Growth, "2011 Annual Report."

36. "Prison: An Economic Boost," *Star-Gazette*, September 20, 1985.

37. Mark Fleisher, "Officially: It's Southport," *Star-Gazette*, 1986.

38. Fleisher, "Officially: It's Southport."

39. See Antonio Gramsci's idea of common sense as ideas that people accept as given in society, as opposed to those which are the result of critical thinking, in Crehan, *Gramsci's Common Sense*.

40. Proceedings of the County Legislature Chemung County, "Resolution Favoring Construction of a 500-Bed Prison Adjacent to the Elmira Correctional Facility."

41. Paul Brooks, "Chemung Doesn't Have Cuomo's Type . . . of Soil," *Star-Gazette*, September 20, 1985.

42. Mark Fleisher, "Benjamin Property Eliminated; 1 Down, 3 to Go on Prison Site," *Star-Gazette*, December 7, 1985.

43. "Prison: An Economic Boost," *Star-Gazette*, September 20, 1985.

44. Fleisher, "Officially: It's Southport."

45. Salle E. Richards, "Town Mourns Loss of Masia," *Star-Gazette*, February 21, 2007.

46. Richards, "Town Mourns Loss of Masia."

47. Fleisher, "Officially: It's Southport."

48. Tom Maguire, "With New Prison, Some Won't Have to Work So Far Away," *Star-Gazette*, December 2, 1985.

49. Phillips-Fein, *Fear City*.

50. Smith and New York State, "In the Matter of a Public Hearing on the Formation of Enterprise Zones in New York State."

51. Smith and New York State, "In the Matter of a Public Hearing on the Formation of Enterprise Zones in New York State."

52. Grant programs shift and change with state and federal elections. Currently in the Southern Tier, businesses have received monies from the Fast NY program, New York Main Street grant, and grants from the regional development corporations called the Consolidated Funding Applications, all of which funnel public capital into smaller scale projects across the state (Chemung County Industrial Development Agency).

53. "Other Applicants for Zone Program," *New York Times*, January 19, 1987.

54. Smith and New York State, "In the Matter of a Public Hearing."

55. Smith and New York State, "In the Matter of a Public Hearing."

56. Pat Louise, "Tug of War Begins for Prison Site," *Star-Gazette,* January 22, 1987.

57. Louise, "Tug of War Begins for Prison Site."

58. Louise, "Tug of War Begins for Prison Site."

59. Editorial Board, "Realities of Third Prison," *Star-Gazette*, January 25, 1987.
60. Editorial Board, "A Nice Nugget for the Tiers," *Star-Gazette*, June 4, 1987.
61. Winant, *Next Shift*; Cowie and Heathcott, *Beyond the Ruins*.

3. Doing My Zero to Eight

1. Lombardo, *Guards Imprisoned*; Pecchio, *The Devil's Den of Prison and Justice*.
2. Schwirtz, Winerip, and Gebeloff, "Scourge of Racial Bias."
3. Burton, *Tip of the Spear*; Khan, "Carceral State," 49–66; Rodriguez, "(Non) Scenes of Captivity," 9–32; Hadden, *Slave Patrols*; Cunha, "Ethnography of Prisons and Penal Confinement," 217–33.
4. Roediger and Esch, *Production of Difference*.
5. Du Bois, *Black Reconstruction in America*, 626.
6. Roediger, *Wages of Whiteness*, 13.
7. See Burton, "To Protect and Serve Whiteness," 38–50; Singh, "The Whiteness of Police," 1091–99.
8. Department of Corrections and Community Supervision New York State, "Incarcerated Profile Report March." There are 363 men who were incarcerated in a county labeled "Upstate other"; 431 in "Upstate urban"; 115 "suburban" New York City; and 480 men from New York City. The county of incarceration simply means where they were convicted of the crime, it does not mean their home county. Nevertheless, I present this data to show that there is a pattern of rural incarceration. See Norton, Pelot-Hobbs, and Schept, *Fighting the New Geography of Mass Incarceration*; Widra and Encalada-Malinowski, "Where People in Prison Come from."
9. Wagner and Kopf, "Racial Geography of Mass Incarceration."
10. New York State Department of Corrections and Community Supervision, "Quarterly Workforce Report." As stated previously, DOCCS declined to give me updated statistics.
11. Schwirtz, Winerip, and Gebeloff, "Scourge of Racial Bias in New York State's Prison."
12. Lombardo, *Guards Imprisoned*.
13. Lombardo, *Guards Imprisoned*, 35.
14. Moskos, *Cop in the Hood*.
15. See also Hill, "Common Enemy Is the Boss and the Inmate," 65–96; Shannon and Page, "Bureaucrats on the Cell Block," 630–57; Page, *Toughest Beat*.
16. Trulia.com, "Elmira Real Estate Market Overview."
17. Formanack's ethnographic work among mobile-home residents in Lincoln, Nebraska, situates this sense of failure in relation to normative whiteness. The author writes succinctly, "Postwar residential segregation, discriminatory lending practices and redlining, and uneven urban development benefitted

white households to such an extent that normative whiteness is identified with middle-class, suburban homeownership." Formanack, "Little White Lies," 95.

18. Pappas, *Magic City*.
19. Berlet and Nemiroff Lyons, *Right-Wing Populism in America*, 2.
20. McMath and Foner, *American Populism*.
21. Stacey, "Finding Dignity in Dirty Work," 831–54.
22. Duvernay, *When They See Us*; Stiller, *Escape at Dannemora*.
23. Norton and Shanahan, "Long Shadow of the Prison Wall."
24. Conover, *Newjack: Guarding Sing Sing*.
25. U.S. Bureau of Labor Statistics, "Labor Force Characteristics by Race and Ethnicity, 2015."
26. Rhodes, *Total Confinement*, 271.

4. Policing the Carceral State

1. The U.S. Census counts incarcerated people in the geographic location where they are incarcerated rather than their home address, thus obfuscating an accurate measure of migration. Considering that New York State incarcerates three times as many African Americans and Latinos than whites in its state prisons, the small number of African Americans who are counted as in-migrants to Chemung County may simply being due to individuals being transferred from another prison. While New York State and Chemung County have opted to remove incarcerated people from their census counts for the purposes of redistricting, the national census continues to count in this manner.
2. U.S. Census Bureau, "U.S. Census Bureau QuickFacts."
3. Hall et al., *Policing the Crisis*, xii.
4. Hall et al., *Policing the Crisis*, xii.
5. U.S. Census Bureau, "U.S. Census Bureau QuickFacts."
6. DeBow, *Statistical View of the United States*; Chemung County Historical Society, "Elmira's African-American Community," 5133.
7. Byrne, "Negro in Elmira," 1747–55.
8. Jim Pfeiffer, "Blame It on the Prisons?" *Star-Gazette*, February 2, 2007.
9. Pfeiffer, "Blame It on the Prisons?"
10. "Five Officers Were Treated at the Hospital after Two Separate Attacks at the Elmira Correctional Facility," Facebook, WENY TV News, June 18, 2021.
11. "Five Officers Were Treated at the Hospital."
12. Pfeiffer, "Blame It on the Prisons?"
13. Salle E. Richards, "Drug Bust Leaves 'Big Dent,'" *Star-Gazette*, August 24, 2007.

14. Editorial board, "Editorial: Operation Crack Hammer a Needed Effort," *Star-Gazette*, August 27, 2007.
15. Richards, "Drug Bust Leaves 'Big Dent.'"
16. Rabuy and Kopf, "Separation by Bars and Miles."
17. Hill, "Common Enemy Is the Boss and the Inmate," 65–96.
18. Harvey, "From Managerialism to Entrepreneurialism," 3–17.
19. Burton, "Fieldnotes on the Gendered Labor of Prison Visitation."
20. Mullings, "Losing Ground," 1–21.
21. Catholic Charities of the Southern Tier, "2007 Homeless Housing Assistance Corporation Report."
22. Burton, *Tip of the Spear*; Berger, *Captive Nation*.
23. This analysis is based on organizational data to which I was given access to during my fieldwork.
24. Seigel, *Violence Work*.
25. Both men who escaped were white men from rural parts of New York State. They were caught after a few days. The fact that these men were white was perhaps a contributing factor in the success of the men's escape and in the fact that they made it as far as they did. Echoing a similar escape from Clinton Correctional Facility in the summer of 2015, I presume white prisoners are more likely to blend in to the local upstate population and remain undetected. It is also likely that white prisoners are treated more leniently and therefore able to garner more trust from rural white guards. See also Schwirtz, Winerip, and Gebeloff, "Scourge of Racial Bias in New York State's Prisons."
26. Jeff Murray, "Panel to Seek Better Ties to Prison," *Star-Gazette*, August 1, 2003.
27. G. Jeffrey Aaron, "Escape Doesn't Faze Prison's Neighbors," *Star-Gazette*, July 8, 2003.

5. *Porous Prison*

1. Berger, *Captive Nation*, 15.
2. Berger, *Captive Nation*.
3. Zach Wheeler and Chelsea Lovell, "NYSCOPBA: Major Uptick of COVID-19 Cases at Elmira Correctional Facility," MyTwinTiers.com, October 2, 2020, https://www.mytwintiers.com/news-cat/breaking-news/nyscopba-major-uptick-of-covid-19-cases-at-elmira-correctional-facility/.
4. "Local Officials: Stop Busing Visitors from Downstate to Elmira Correctional Facility," MyTwinTiers.com, October 7, 2020, https://www.mytwintiers.com/video/local-officials-stop-busing-visitors-from-downstate-to-elmira-correctional-facility/5916427.

5. "Elmira Correctional Facility Visitor Speaks Out Against Reason for Limiting Visitation," *WENY News*, October 8, 2020, https://www.weny.com/story/42742836/elmira-correctional-facility-visitor-speaks-out-against-reason-for-limiting-visitation.

6. Vaccination rates of 28 percent were reported in April of 2021 (Iverac) and 59 percent November 2021 (Alba); Mirela Iverac, "Less Than a Third of NY Prison Staff Vaccinated against COVID," *Gothamist*, June 8, 2021, https://gothamist.com/news/less-third-ny-prison-staff-vaccinated-against-covid; Fernando Alba, "Latest Vaccine Incentive for COs: Beards, Colored Nails," *Press-Republican*, November 25, 2021, https://www.pressrepublican.com/news/local_news/latest-vaccine-incentive-for-cos-beards-colored-nails/article_0004c9ad-8732-5aa2-a267-33ab46045ac9.html.

7. Chemung County Department of Health, "Chemung County Covid-19 Complaints."

8. Kauffman, "Why Jails Are Key to 'Flattening the Curve' of Coronavirus."

9. Marquez et al., "COVID-19 Incidence and Mortality in Federal and State Prisons," 1865.

10. Jillian Forstadt, "New Yorkers in 4 Cities Protest, as Elmira Prison Hits 565 COVID-19 Cases," *WBFO, NPR*, October 28, 2020, https://www.wbfo.org/crime/2020-10-28/new-yorkers-in-4-cities-protest-as-elmira-prison-hits-565-covid-19-cases.

11. Forstadt, "New Yorkers in 4 Cities Protest."

12. Fisher, "Remarks by Commissioner Brian Fischer."

13. Boulin Johnson, Todd, and Subramanian, "Violence in Police Families," 3–12.

14. Lutz, *Homefront*.

15. Conover, *Newjack*, 245.

16. Philliber, "Thy Brother's Keeper," 9–37.

17. The Correctional Association of New York, "Solitary at Southport"; Siennick et al., "Revisiting and Unpacking the Mental Illness and Solitary Confinement Relationship," 772–801; Reiter et al., "Psychological Distress in Solitary Confinement," s56–62.

18. Ben-Moshe, *Decarcerating Disability*.

6. Prison Visiting in a Prison Town

1. Video viewed by author on VHS in home of Irene, May 2008.

Conclusion

1. Roediger, *History Against Misery*, xi.

2. Burton, *Tip of the Spear*; Camp and Heatherton, *Policing the Planet*; Hinton, *From the War on Poverty to the War on Crime*.
3. Berger, Kaba, and Stein, "What Abolitionists Do."
4. Conover, *Newjack*; Huling, "Building a Prison Economy in Rural America," 197–213.

Bibliography

Archives and Manuscript Materials

City of Ogdensburg, Department of Planning and Development. "City of Ogdensburg, Economic Development Zone, 1987 Annual Report." Ogdensburg NY, January 18, 1989. NYS Archives, Enterprize Zones, Box #4.

Published Works

Aiken, Joshua. "Era of Mass Expansion: Why State Officials Should Fight Jail Growth." Report, Prison Policy Initiative, 2017. https://www.prisonpolicy .org/reports/jailsovertime.html.

Alexander, Michelle. *The New Jim Crow: Mass Incarceration in the Age of Color-blindness*. New York: The New Press, 2010.

Benavides, A. J. "Elmira Reformatory." In *Encyclopedia of Crime and Punishment*, edited by D. Levinson, 1126–28. Thousand Oaks CA: SAGE, 2002.

Ben-Moshe, Liat. *Decarcerating Disability: Deinstitutionalization and Prison Abolition*. Minneapolis: University of Minnesota Press, 2020.

Berger, Dan. *Captive Nation: Black Prison Organizing in the Civil Rights Era*. Justice, Power, and Politics. Chapel Hill: University of North Carolina Press, 2014.

Berger, Dan, Mariame Kaba, and David Stein. "What Abolitionists Do." *Jacobin* 24 (2017).

Berlet, Chip, and Matthew Nemiroff Lyons. *Right-Wing Populism in America: Too Close for Comfort*. Critical Perspectives. New York: Guilford Press, 2000.

"Beyond the Prison Industrial Complex." Chicago, October 26, 2011. YouTube video. https://www.youtube.com/watch?v=stpjC-7edkc&ab_channel= cantv.

Bonds, Anne. "Economic Development, Racialization, and Privilege: 'Yes in My Backyard' Prison Politics and the Reinvention of Madras, Oregon." *Annals of the Association of American Geographers* 103, no. 6 (April 2013): 1389–1405.

———. "Profit from Punishment? The Politics of Prisons, Poverty and Neoliberal Restructuring in the Rural American Northwest." *Antipode* 38, no. 1 (2006): 174–77.

Burch, Melissa. "Scripting the Conviction: Power and Resistance in the Management of Criminal Stigma." *American Anthropologist* 123, no. 3 (September 2021): 645–57.

Burton, Orisanmi. "Fieldnotes on the Gendered Labor of Prison Visitation." *Anthropoliteia* (blog), November 10, 2015. https://anthropoliteia.net/2015 /11/10/fieldnotes-on-the-gendered-labor-of-prison-visitation/.

———. "The Minimum Demands." *New York History* 102, no. 1 (2021): 13–16.

———. *Tip of the Spear: Black Radicalism, Prison Repression, and the Long Attica Revolt*. Berkeley: University of California Press, 2023.

———. "To Protect and Serve Whiteness: To Protect and Serve Whiteness." *North American Dialogue* 18, no. 2 (October 2015): 38–50.

Byrne, Tom. "The Negro in Elmira: Black History." *Chemung County Historical Journal* 14, no. 1 (1968): 1747–55.

Camp, Jordan T., and Christina Heatherton, eds. *Policing the Planet: Why the Policing Crisis Led to Black Lives Matter*. New York: Verso, 2016.

Casanova, Ron. *Each One Teach One*. Edited by Steven Blackburn. Evanston IL: Curbstone Press, 1996.

Catholic Charities of the Southern Tier. "2007 Homeless Housing Assistance Corporation Report." 2007.

Center for Behavioral Health Statistics and Quality. "National Survey on Drug Use and Health (NSDUH): Summary of Methodological Studies, 1971–2014." Rockville MA: Substance Abuse and Mental Health Services Administration, 2015.

Chemung County Department of Health. "Chemung County Covid-19 Complaints." Chemung County NY. https://www.chemungcountyny.gov /chemung_county_covid-19_complaints/index.php.

Chemung County Historical Society. "Elmira's African-American Community." *Chemung County Historical Journal* 47, no. 1 (2001): 5133.

Chemung County IDA. "Chemung County Industrial Development Agency Meeting Minutes." Elmira, New York: Chemung County Industrial Development Agency, January 11, 2024.

City of Elmira. "City of Elmira, Budget Worksheet Proposed." November 21, 2022.

Conover, Ted. *Newjack: Guarding Sing Sing*. New York: Random House, 2000.

Correctional Association of New York, The. "Solitary at Southport." New York, 2017. https://static1.squarespace.com/static/5b2c07e2a9e02851fb387477 /t/5c4f5bd8562fa7fb256b550d/1548704749745/2017+Solitary+at +Southport.pdf.

Coughlin, Thomas. "Report of Operations and Development 1980–1981." Department of Corrections New York State, 1981.

Cowie, Jefferson, and Joseph Heathcott, eds. *Beyond the Ruins: The Meanings of Deindustralization*. Ithaca NY: Cornell University Press, 2003.

Crehan, Kate. *Gramsci's Common Sense: Inequality and Its Narratives*. Durham NC: Duke University Press, 2016.

Cronon, William. *Nature's Metropolis: Chicago and the Great West*. New York: W. W. Norton, 1992.

Cunha, Manuela. "The Ethnography of Prisons and Penal Confinement." *Annual Review of Anthropology* 43, no. 1 (October 2014): 217–33.

Department of Corrections and Community Supervision New York State. "Incarcerated Profile Report March." Albany NY: Department of Corrections and Community Supervision New York State, March 2024. https://doccs.ny.gov /system/files/documents/2024/03/2024_03_01-uc-profile.pdf.

Driscoll, Barbara A. *The Tracks North: The Railroad Bracero Program of World War II*. Austin: University of Texas Press, 1999.

Du Bois, W.E.B. *Black Reconstruction in America: 1860–1880*. New York: Free Press, 1998.

DuVernay, Eva, prod. *When They See Us*. 2019. Netflix.Eason, John Major. *Big House on the Prairie: Rise of the Rural Ghetto and Prison Proliferation*. Chicago: University of Chicago Press, 2017.

Findlay, Eileen. *We Are Left without a Father Here: Masculinity, Domesticity, and Migration in Postwar Puerto Rico*. American Encounters/Global Interactions. Durham NC: Duke University Press, 2014.

Fisher, Brian. "Remarks by Commissioner Brian Fischer, Graduating Correction Officer Class Albany Training Academy." http://www.doccs.ny.gov /Commissioner/Speeches/classof08.html.

Flores, Lori A. *Grounds for Dreaming: Mexican Americans, Mexican Immigrants, and the California Farmworker Movement*. New Haven: Yale University Press, 2016.

Formanack, Allison. "Little White Lies: Hope and Untruth in (White) Mobile-Homeownership." *Journal for the Anthropology of North America* 25, no. 2 (October 2022): 94–113.

García-Colón, Ismael. *Colonial Migrants at the Heart of Empire: Puerto Rican Workers on U.S. Farms*. American Crossroads 57. Oakland: University of California Press, 2020.

Gilmore, Ruth Wilson. "Beyond the Prison Industrial Complex." Lecture, Chicago Access Network Television, October 26, 2011. Available on YouTube video. https://youtu.be/sTPjC-7EDkc?si=QAdT9mMLrxfW8074.

———. "Extraction: Abolition Geography and the Problem of Innocence." Presented at the Institute for Geographies of Justice, University of the Witwatersrand, Johannesburg, South Africa, June 22, 2015. https://www.wits.ac .za/news/latest-news/general-news/2015/2015–06/radical-geographer -at-wits.html.

———. "Globalisation and US Prison Growth: From Military Keynesianism to Post-Keynesian Militarism." *Race & Class* 40, no. 2–3 (March 1999): 171–88.

———. *Golden Gulag: Prisons, Surplus, Crisis, and Opposition in Globalizing California*. Berkeley: University of California Press, 2006.

Goffman, Erving. *Asylums: Essays on the Social Situation of Mental Patients and Other Inmates*. London: Taylor and Francis, 2017.

Gray, M. P. *The Business of Captivity: Elmira and Its Civil War Prison*. Kent: Kent State University Press, 2001.

Hadden, Sally E. *Slave Patrols: Law and Violence in Virginia and the Carolinas*. Cambridge MA: Harvard University Press, 2003.

Hahamovitch, Cindy. *No Man's Land: Jamaican Guestworkers in America and the Global History of Deportable Labor*. Politics and Society in Twentieth-Century America. Princeton NJ: Princeton University Press, 2011.

Hall, Stuart, Chas Chritcher, Tony Jefferson, John Clarke, and Brian Roberts. *Policing the Crisis: Mugging, the State, and Law and Order*. 2nd ed. Houndmills, Basingstoke, Hampshire: Palgrave Macmillan, 2013.

Hart, Richard. *Towards Decolonisation: Political, Labour and Economic Developments in Jamaica 1938–1945*. UWI Press Political History Series 3. Kingston, Jamaica: Canoe Press, University of the West Indies, 1999.

Harvey, David. *The Condition of Postmodernity*. Malden MA: Blackwell, 1989.

———. "From Managerialism to Entrepreneurialism: The Transformation in Urban Governance in Late Capitalism." *Geografiska Annaler* 71, no. 1 (1989): 3–17.

Hill, Rebecca. "The Common Enemy Is the Boss and the Inmate: Police and Prison Guard Unions in New York in the 1970s–1980s." *Labor* 8, no. 3 (2011): 65–96.

Hinton, Elizabeth Kai. *From the War on Poverty to the War on Crime: The Making of Mass Incarceration in America*. Cambridge MA: Harvard University Press, 2016.

Hooks, Gregory, Clayton Mosher, Thomas Rotolo, and Linda Lobao. "The Prison Industry: Carceral Expansion and Employment in U.S. Counties, 1969–1994*." *Social Science Quarterly* 85, no. 1 (March 2004): 37–57.

Horigan, Michael. *Elmira: Death Camp of the North*. Mechanicsburg PA: Stackpole Books, 2002.

HoSang, Daniel, and Joseph E. Lowndes. *Producers, Parasites, Patriots: Race and the New Right-Wing Politics of Precarity*. Minneapolis: University of Minnesota Press, 2019.

Huling, Tracy. "Building a Prison Economy in Rural America." In *Invisible Punishment: The Collateral Consequences of Mass Imprisonment*, edited by Meda Chesney-Lind, and Marc Mauer, 197–213. New York: New Press, 2002.

Hyatt, Sue. "What Was Neoliberalism and What Comes Next?" In *Policy Worlds: Anthropology and the Analysis of Contemporary Power*, edited by Cris Shore, Susan Wright, and David Peró, 105–24. New York: Berghahn Books, 2011.

Johnson, Leanor Boulin, Michael Todd, and Ganga Subramanian. "Violence in Police Families: Work-Family Spillover." *Journal of Family Violence* 20, no. 1 (February 2005): 3–12.

Kasinitz, Philip. *Caribbean New York: Black Immigrants and the Politics of Race*. Anthropology of Contemporary Issues. Ithaca NY: Cornell University Press, 1992.

Kasmir, Sharryn. "The Mondragón Model as Post-Fordist Discourse: Considerations on the Production of Post-Fordism." *Critique of Anthropology* 19, no. 4 (December 1999): 379–400.

Kauffman, Kelsey. "Why Jails Are Key to 'Flattening the Curve' of Coronavirus." *Appeal* (blog), March 13, 2020. https://theappeal.org/jails-coronavirus-covid -19-pandemic-flattening-curve/.

Khan, Aisha. "The Carceral State: An American Story." *Annual Review of Anthropology* 51, no. 1 (October 2022): 49–66.

Logan, John R., and Harvey Molotch. *Urban Fortunes: The Political Economy of Place, 20th Anniversary Edition, with a New Preface*. Berkeley: University of California Press, 2007.

Lombardo, Lucian. *Guards Imprisoned: Correctional Officers at Work*. New York: Elsevier, 1998.

Lutz, Catherine A. *Homefront: A Military City and the American Twentieth Century*. Boston: Beacon Press, 2001.

Manuel-Scott, Wendi N. "Soldiers of the Field: Jamaican Farm Workers in the United States During World War II." PhD diss., Howard University, 2003.

Marquez, Neal, Julie A. Ward, Kalind Parish, Brendan Saloner, and Sharon Dolovich. "COVID-19 Incidence and Mortality in Federal and State Prisons Compared with the US Population, April 5, 2020, to April 3, 2021." *JAMA* 326, no. 18 (November 2021): 1865.

Martin, Laura Renata. "Historicizing White Nostalgia: Race and American Fordism." *Blindfield Journal* (blog), August 3, 2017. https://blindfieldjournal.com /2017/08/03/historicizing-white-nostalgia-race-and-american-fordism/.

Marx, Karl. *The Eighteenth Brumaire of Louis Napoleon*. Gloucester UK: Dodo Press, 2009.

McMath, Robert C., and Eric Foner. *American Populism: A Social History, 1877– 1898*. New York: Hill and Wang, 1993.

Melamed, Jodi. "Racial Capitalism." *Critical Ethnic Studies* 1, no. 1 (2015): 76–85.

Molina, Natalia. *How Race Is Made in America: Immigration, Citizenship, and the Historical Power of Racial Scripts*. Berkeley: University of California Press, 2014.

Morrell, Andrea. "'Municipal Welfare' and the Neoliberal Prison Town: The Political Economy of Prison Closures in New York State." *North American Dialogue* 2, no. 15 (2012): 43–49.

———. "Policing the Carceral State: Prisons and Panic in an Upstate New York Prison Town." *Transforming Anthropology* 26, no. 1 (April 2018): 50–62.

———. "Hometown Prison: Whiteness, Safety, and Prison Work in Upstate New York State." *American Anthropologist* 123, no. 3 (September 2021): 633–44.

Moskos, Peter. *Cop in the Hood: My Year Policing Baltimore's Eastern District.* Princeton NJ: Princeton University Press, 2008.

Muehlebach, Andrea, and Nitzan Shoshan. "Introduction." *Anthropological Quarterly* 85, no. 2 (2012): 317–43.

Mullings, Leith. "Losing Ground." *Souls* 5, no. 2 (June 2003): 1–21.

———. *On Our Own Terms: Race, Class, and Gender in the Lives of African-American Women.* Hoboken NJ: Taylor and Francis, 2014.

Murakawa, Naomi. *The First Civil Right: How Liberals Built Prison America.* New York: Oxford University Press, 2014.

Narayan, Kirin. "How Native Is a 'Native' Anthropologist?" *American Anthropologist*, no. 3 (1993): 671–86.

New York State Corrections and Community Supervision. "Under Custody Report: Profile of Under Custody Population as of January 1, 2021." Albany NY. https://doccs.ny.gov/system/files/documents/2022/04/under-custody-report-for-2021.pdf.

New York State Department of Corrections and Community Supervision. "Quarterly Workforce Report: Ethnic and Sexual Breakdown." Albany NY: New York State Department of Correctional Service, 2008.

New York State Department of Corrections and Community Supervision and Kim Dworakowski. "Under Custody Report: Profile of Under Custody Population as of January 1, 2017." Albany NY, April 2017. http://www.doccs.ny.gov/Research/Reports/2017/Under%20custody%20report%202017.pdf.

New York State Department of Corrections of Community Supervision. "DOCCS Fact Sheet: January 1, 2021." https://doccs.ny.gov/system/files/documents/2021/01/doccs-fact-sheet-january-2021.pdf.

Norton, Jack. "Little Siberia, Star of the North." In *Historical Geographies of Prisons: Unlocking the Usable Carceral Past*, edited by Dominique Moran and Karen Morin, 168–84. New York: Routledge, 2015.

Norton, Jack. "'We Are Not Going to Rest': Organizing against Incarceration in Upstate New York." *In Our Backyards Stories* (blog), September 3, 2019. https://www.vera.org/in-our-backyards-stories/we-are-not-going-to-rest.

Norton, Jack, Lydia Pelot-Hobbs, and Judah Nathan Schept, eds. *The Jail Is Everywhere: Fighting the New Geography of Mass Incarceration.* New York: Verso, 2024.

Norton, Jack, and Jarrod Shanahan. "The Long Shadow of the Prison Wall." Jacobinmag.com. *Jacobin* (blog), January 8, 2019. https://www.jacobinmag .com/2019/01/escape-at-dannemora-joyce-mitchell-sweat-prisons.

Omi, Michael, and Howard Winant. *Racial Formation in the United States: From the 1960s to the 1990s*. 2nd ed. New York: Routledge, 1994.

Page, Joshua. *The Toughest Beat: Politics, Punishment, and the Prison Officers Union in California*. Oxford: Oxford University Press, 2013.

Paoline, Eugene A. "Police Culture." In *Encyclopedia of Criminology and Criminal Justice*, edited by Gerben Bruinsma and David Weisburd, 3577–86. New York: Springer New York, 2014.

Pappas, Gregory. *The Magic City: Unemployment in a Working-Class Community*. Anthropology of Contemporary Issues. Ithaca NY: Cornell University Press, 1989.

Pecchio, John J. *The Devil's Den of Prison and Justice*. Binghamton NY: Brundage, 2006.

Pelot-Hobbs, Lydia. *Prison Capital: Mass Incarceration and Struggles for Abolition Democracy in Louisiana*. Justice, Power, and Politics. Chapel Hill: University of North Carolina Press, 2023.

Philliber, Susan. "Thy Brother's Keeper: A Review of the Literature on Correctional Officers." *Justice Quarterly* 4, no. 1 (March 1987): 9–37.

Phillips-Fein, Kim. *Fear City: New York's Fiscal Crisis and the Rise of Austerity Politics*. New York: Metropolitan Books, 2017.

Pisciotta, Alexander W. *Benevolent Repression: Social Control and the American Reformatory-Prison Movement*. New York: New York University Press, 1994.

Price, Joshua M. *Prison and Social Death*. Critical Issues in Crime and Society. New Brunswick NJ: Rutgers University Press, 2015.

Proceedings of the County Legislature Chemung County. Proceedings of the County Legislature Chemung County, 85–171 § (1985).

Pyle, Kevin, and Craig Gilmore. *Prison Town: Paying the Price*. Real Cost of Prisons Project. Northampton MA: Real Cost of Prisons Project, 2005.

Rabuy, Bernadette, and Daniel Kopf. "Separation by Bars and Miles: Visitation in State Prisons." Prison Policy Initiative, October 20, 2015. https://www .prisonpolicy.org/reports/prisonvisits.html.

Reiter, Keramet, Joseph Ventura, David Lovell, Dallas Augustine, Melissa Barragan, Thomas Blair, Kelsie Chesnut, et al. "Psychological Distress in Solitary Confinement: Symptoms, Severity, and Prevalence in the United States, 2017–2018." *American Journal of Public Health* 110, no. s1 (January 2020): s56–62.

Rhodes, Lorna A. *Total Confinement: Madness and Reason in the Maximum-Security Prison*. California Series in Public Anthropology 7. Berkeley: University of California Press, 2004.

Robinson, Cedric J. *Black Marxism: The Making of the Black Radical Tradition*. Chapel Hill: University of North Carolina Press, 1983.

Robinson, Cedric J., H. L. T. Quan, Ruth Wilson Gilmore, and Elizabeth Peters Robinson. *Cedric J. Robinson: On Racial Capitalism, Black Internationalism, and Cultures of Resistance*. Black Critique. London: Pluto Press, 2019.

Rodriguez, D. "(Non)Scenes of Captivity: The Common Sense of Punishment and Death." *Radical History Review* 2006, no. 96 (October 1, 2006): 9–32.

Roediger, David R. *History against Misery*. Chicago: Charles Kerr, 2006.

———. *The Wages of Whiteness: Race and the Making of the American Working Class*. Haymarket Series. London: Verso, 1991.

———. *Working toward Whiteness: How America's Immigrants Became White: The Strange Journey from Ellis Island to the Suburbs*. 2nd edition. New York: Basic Books, 2018.

Roediger, David R., and Elizabeth D. Esch. *The Production of Difference: Race and the Management of Labor in U.S. History*. New York: Oxford University Press, 2012.

Roseberry, William. "Hegemony and the Language of Contention." In *In Everyday Forms of State Formation: Revolution and the Negotiation of Rule in Modern Mexico*, edited by Gilbert Joseph and Daniel Nugent, 355–66. Durham NC: Duke University Press, 1994.

———. "Political Economy." *Annual Review of Anthropology* 17 (1988): 161–85.

Schept, Judah. *Coal, Cages, Crisis: The Rise of the Prison Economy in Central Appalachia*. New York: New York University Press, 2022.

———. *Progressive Punishment: Job Loss, Jail Growth, and the Neoliberal Logic of Carceral Expansion*. Alternative Criminology Series. New York: New York University Press, 2015.

Seigel, Micol. *Violence Work: State Power and the Limits of Police*. Durham NC: Duke University Press, 2018.

Shannon, Sarah K. S., and Joshua Page. "Bureaucrats on the Cell Block: Prison Officers' Perceptions of Work Environment and Attitudes toward Prisoners." *Social Service Review* 88, no. 4 (December 2014): 630–57.

Shore, Cris, Susan Wright, and Davide Però, eds. *Policy Worlds: Anthropology and the Analysis of Contemporary Power*. EASA Series, vol. 14. New York: Berghahn Books, 2011.

Siennick, Sonja E., Mayra Picon, Jennifer M. Brown, and Daniel P. Mears. "Revisiting and Unpacking the Mental Illness and Solitary Confinement Relationship." *Justice Quarterly* 39, no. 4 (June 2022): 772–801.

Singh, Nikhil Pal. "The Whiteness of Police." *American Quarterly* 66, no. 4 (2014): 1091–99.

Smith, A. Lynn, and Anna Eisenstein. *Rebuilding Shattered Worlds: Creating Community by Voicing the Past*. Lincoln: University of Nebraska Press, 2016.

Smith, Neil. *The New Urban Frontier: Gentrification and the Revanchist City*. New York: Routledge, 1996.

Smith, William T., and New York State. "In the Matter of a Public Hearing on the Formation of Enterprise Zones in New York State [Held in] Chemung County Legislative Chambers, 205 Lake Street, Elmira, New York." Senate Majority Task Force on Business Retention and Expansion, February 20, 1986.

Southern Tier Economic Growth. "2011 Annual Report." Southern Tier Economic Growth, 2011.

Stacey, Clare L. "Finding Dignity in Dirty Work: The Constraints and Rewards of Low-Wage Home Care Labour." *Sociology of Health and Illness* 27, no. 6 (September 2005): 831–54.

Stiller, Ben, dir. 2019. *Escape at Dannemora*. Hollywood, California: Paramount.

Sugrue, Thomas J. *The Origins of the Urban Crisis: Race and Inequality in Postwar Detroit*. Princeton Studies in American Politics: Historical, International, and Comparative Perspectives. Princeton NJ: Princeton University Press, 2014.

Susser, Ida. "Tracing the Critical in Urban Anthropology." *City & Society* 34, no. 1 (April 2022): 18–23.

Tese, Vincent. "Rebuilding New York: The New Phase—From Recovery to Resurgence: A Strategic Plan for Expanding Economic and Job Development in New York State." Albany NY: Office of Economic Development, September 30, 1985.

Trulia.com. "Elmira Real Estate Market Overview." Accessed October 18, 2024. https://www.trulia.com/real_estate/Elmira-New_York/.

United States and J. D. B. De Bow. *The Seventh Census of the United States, 1850 : Embracing a Statistical View of Each of the States and Territories . . .* Washington DC: R. Armstrong, 1853.

United States Tariff Commission. "Calculators, Typewriters, and Typewriter Parts: Workers of the Remington Rand Division, Sperry Rand Corporation, Report to the President on Investigation no. TEA-W-140 Under Section 301(c)(2) of the Trade Expansion Act of 1962." Washington DC: United States Tariff Commission, June 1972. https://www.usitc.gov/publications/tea/pub492.pdf.

U.S. Bureau of Labor Statistics. "Labor Force Characteristics by Race and Ethnicity, 2015." U.S. Department of Justice Office of Justice Programs Bureau of Justice Statistics, September 2016. http://www.bls.gov/opub/reports/race-and-ethnicity/2015/pdf/home.pdf.

U.S. Census Bureau. "U.S. Census Bureau QuickFacts: Elmira City, New York." 2010.

———. "U.S. Census Bureau QuickFacts: Elmira City, New York." 2023. https://www.census.gov/quickfacts/fact/table/elmiracitynewyork/pst045222.

Vera Institute of Justice. "Empire State of Incarceration." New York, February 18, 2021. https://www.vera.org/empire-state-of-incarceration-2021#people-in-prison-in-new-york-state.

Wacquant, Loïc. "Deadly Symbiosis: When Ghetto and Prison Meet and Mesh." *Punishment & Society* 3, no. 1 (January 2001): 95–133.

Wagner, Peter, and Daniel Kopf. "The Racial Geography of Mass Incarceration." Prison Policy Initiative, July 2015.

Wagner, Peter, Megan Rudy, Ellie Happel, and William Goldberg. "Phantom Constituents in the Empire State: How Outdated Census Bureau Methodology Burdens New York Counties." Northampton MA: Prison Policy Initiative, Prisoners of the Census, 2007. https://www.prisonersofthecensus.org/nycounties/report.html.

Wakefield, Sara, and Christopher James Wildeman. *Children of the Prison Boom: Mass Incarceration and the Future of American Inequality*. Studies in Crime and Public Policy. Oxford: Oxford University Press, 2014.

Waldram, James. "Anthropology in Prison: Negotiating Consent and Accountability with a 'Captured' Population." *Human Organization* 57, no. 2 (June 1998): 238–44.

Widra, Emily, and Nick Encalada-Malinowski. "Where People in Prison Come From: The Geography of Mass Incarceration in New York." Northampton MA: Prison Policy Initiative, 2022. https://www.prisonpolicy.org/origin/ny/2020/report.html.

Williams, Karen. "From Coercion to Consent?: Governing the Formerly Incarcerated in the 21st Century United States." PhD diss., CUNY Graduate Center, 20216.

Willis, Paul. *Learning to Labor: How Working-Class Kids Get Working Class Jobs*. New York: Columbia University Press, 1977.

Winant, Gabriel. *The Next Shift: The Fall of Industry and the Rise of Health Care in Rust Belt America*. Cambridge MA: Harvard University Press, 2021.

Woods, Clyde. *Development Arrested: The Blues and Plantation Power in the Mississippi Delta*. New York: Verso Books, 2017.

Index

Southport, Town of, 38, 55–58, 64

Southport Correctional Facility, 2, 8, 19, 26, 38; construction as a Supermax Prison, 8; uprising of 1991, 18; use of solitary for prisoners with mental health diagnoses, 122

Southside of Elmira, 8, 38

Star-Gazette: Black church member obituaries, 30; editorial support for prison expansion, 54, 60; "MK Smykowski, Rand Retiree" obituary, 27; Remington Rand worker obituaries, 29

Steele Memorial Library, 43

STEG (Southern Tier Economic Growth), 52–57

Strategic Plan for Economic Development in New York State (1985), 50

strike: of CIO unions (1946), 35; of corrections officers, 16.

Sugrue, Tom, 31

tax abatements, as part of enterprise zones, 44, 50, 59–61

Tese, Vincent, 44, 50–51, 60–61. *See also* Urban Development Corporation (UDC)

the unemployed, advocates for, 60

unemployment, as a result of deindustrialization, 39–42

uneven development, 7, 9

United Electrical, Radio, and Machine Workers Local 310 of the CIO, 35

Upstate, uses of, 63–64

Urban Development Corporation (UDC), 9, 43–44, 49–52

urban renewal, 86

urban/rural divide in prisons, 13

U.S. Steel, American Bridge Works, 15

Veteran, Town of, as potential site of prison, 55

volunteers, at Elmira Reception Center, 19

Wacquant, Loic, 7

War Manpower Commission, 35

When They See Us (Duvarnay), 77

whiteness, 4, 13–14, 30–31, 39, 67; and W. E. B. Du Bois's "psychological wage," 14

Winner, George, 55–56, 61–62

working class: and formations of whiteness, 13, 25; and nostalgia for factory work, 32; and racial divisions, 24, 28–31, 33; and social organizations, 31

WPA (Works Progress Administration), 29

To order or obtain more
information on these or other
University of Nebraska Press titles,
visit nebraskapress.unl.edu.

www.ingramcontent.com/pod-product-compliance
Lightning Source LLC
Chambersburg PA
CBHW030334270326
41926CB00010B/1620